ERA ZISTEL *The Gentle People*

Illustrated by Matthew Kalmenoff

HOLT, RINEHART AND WINSTON
New York · Chicago · San Francisco

Other versions of some of the stories in this volume
have appeared in *Audubon, Down East, Everywoman,* and
The Saturday Evening Post.

First Edition

Designed by Ernst Reichl
89886-0214
Printed in the United States of America

The Gentle People

Books by Era Zistel

Wintertime Cat
The Good Year
Orphan, a Raccoon
Golden Book of Cat Stories
Treasury of Cat Stories
Golden Book of Dog Stories
Hänsel und Gretel (Germany)

On occasion a woman will say to me, in some short interval between denying, admonishing, threatening, screaming, yanking, punishing, and wiping the runny noses of her contribution to the human explosion, "Ah, but no children," then shake her head commiseratively or nod knowingly, thus implying, or even audibly suggesting, that this sad lack must be the reason for my otherwise unaccountable love for animals. She couldn't be more in error; the way I have invested the second best life given me has not been second choice. Clicking her tongue, this same dogmatist might add, "But what a shame to waste all that money," as if, having squandered my life, I ought to at least refrain from doing the same with my meager funds.

Although it may not merit consideration, I have thought a good deal about such criticism, and in the last analysis it seems to me almost sacrilegious; an expression of opinion that, in making some of us love animals, God has been in grievous error. Since they have been put here, and man's uncontrolled, unconcerned swarming has made existence for anything else on this earth nearly impossible without his help, obviously someone must take care of animals. Those of us who do, in large part or small, are merely an essential part of an immensely complex whole. To question our function is to discredit all creation.

At some time or other all of us, even the lowliest, must come to wonder why we were born, what purpose we fulfill beyond elemental self-preservation and procreation. There was a day long ago, when I approached my mother, as she did the week's wash in the basement, with what was to me a momentous proposition. Could I convert a part of that basement, just one corner, into a studio? All I needed was such a retreat, a table, a desk lamp, our typewriter, and I would write a great book. I must have been very young, for the scene is dimly lit in memory; and one of the poignant convictions of youth seems to be that, give proper accouterment, any goal is attainable. My mother nodded gravely, but must have laughed inside with pity; she was old enough to know how inherent limitations proscribe ambition.

After about five pages had been written in small assured script, which I kept in my files for years to provide occasional nostalgic amusement, my sights shifted. No, instead I would be another Pavlova: a great, great dancer. As a student I wasn't too bad as long as I managed to stay on my feet. Too often there'd be a thud; the eyes of the whole class would swivel, knowing exactly where to look, and in the back row, fourth from the left, Era would be sprawled again. Our instructor shook his abundant hair, sputtered in Russian, and searched his closet for another pair of slippers my size. But we both knew it wasn't the slippers; I simply was no dancer.

I joined a class in sculpture, at the end of the day stared long at the beauty of the Negro model, looked with revelatory detachment at what I had made of him, and stole away.

The theater beckoned. Again I became a pupil, studying with a lovely woman who at long last became too aware of her own limitations and jumped out of a window; thus following, in a way, the dancing instructor who, after watching Martha Graham, leaped over Niagara Falls. The dramatic coach has my gratitude. She gave me a reasonably graceful walk, toes in, not out; lowered my voice an octave, got rid of the strident Midwestern accent, loosened my joints, taught me to fall without hurting myself—now an invaluable and much used gift. In fact

2

she made me over completely, but of course she could not create. The spark was not in me.

I thought it was. From her rigorous discipline I graduated to a job in a little theater, originally a burlesque house, converted because the owner's wife had social ambitions. How could she ascend the insecure ladder of good breeding if her husband made his money offering sagging flesh and stale jokes to a raucous public? Better he should lose it, which he did. During the day I worked in the office, but each enchanted evening I entered dazzling, scented unreality to emote in Shakespeare, Molière, Wilde, and Sheridan, while die-hards in the audience, not believing in the reformation, yelled, "Take it off! Take it off!"

When at last the owner had got rid of all his tainted money and I was forty dollars ahead, I went with that sum pinned inside my blouse to Chicago and worked in stock, until one day that city's infamous wind picked up my ninety-six pounds like a scrap of wastepaper and had great sport tossing it about for half a block. Through the bout of pneumonia that followed, I was cared for by the only doctor willing to make a night call. He turned out to be a dope addict, but a fine, dedicated, conscientious fellow who scarcely left my bedside during the first few critical days and nights. I think of that man, who, if not mercifully dead, must be languishing in some dive similar to the one I learned he lived in then, with regret that I have not fully utilized the additional years of life he gave me.

Recovered, I trembled through a daily session of mike fright on a radio program, then took the citadel of New York City by doldrum, making the rounds of casting offices along with hundreds just like me, meanwhile paying the landlord, the butcher and the grocer by modeling. Somewhere there still may be a sculptured madonna wearing my head, but my legs in the newspaper ads must have been wrapped long since around a day's accumulation of garbage.

In middle youth one becomes most acutely aware of the passage of time, the need to hurry toward something other than routine old age. Where was I, I asked myself, and why? I didn't know. For years I didn't know, until I faced up to inflexible reality: there is no greatness in me, none at all. I am small and   3 can do only small things. I hold in my hands an insignificant, terrified, desperate sickness, give what relief is in my power, either renewed being or non-being, and no longer question my purpose. Tomorrow's death can be met with equanimity because today I have been not entirely useless.

I was racketing around in Harlem, having a wonderful time and hating life, when I met Eric. At first I didn't like him; then I liked him a little; then I was in love, for the first time and, as it turned out, the last. We found a place to live on the outskirts of Greenwich Village, in a brownstone house so old it was measured every so often to discover how much closer it had come to expiration in its last long sigh. Below us dwelled some people we never saw who evidently possessed only one record and played it every evening. Even now, whenever I hear *Prince Igor,* I am momentarily transported to that small apartment, Eric seated across from me at the long oak table, tapping on his typewriter with the two newspaper-trained fingers; and Cleo, who disapproved of my housekeeping, washing the table leg at my feet. Above us lived a man who now and then gave himself too large a dose of heroin and went berserk, once falling over the stair rail to land just outside our door. His wife, a "masseuse," went out each night carrying a little black satchel, and returned at dawn. On the one side was another man with a wife who became his daughter whenever she had a date. The walls were thin. "Good night, Daddy," we'd hear her say, and her husband would answer complacently, "Goodnight, daughter. Don't stay out too late." On the other side lived the landlord with all his dogs.

In our apartment Eric and I worked together on translations, rewrites, ghost jobs, anything that came along to give us daily bread, coasting pleasantly along a life of no particular commitment or design, until one morning I happened to look out of the window and there, in the littered courtyard two stories down, was destiny. She wore a coat that was dirty white, except for two black spots like clown's eyebrows on either side of her head; her eyes were brilliant green, and sad. She tipped up her head to stare at me; I leaned out of the window to look down at her, and no word passed between us. Then the following day I saw her again, not in the courtyard but on the window ledge, a precarious perch she had reached by climbing two flights of the fire ladder's slippery rungs. When Eric came home that afternoon I said, "We have a cat." Two days later I said, "We have three cats."

On that day, Cleo had grunted and heaved and screamed, but could not give birth. I had to help her. Kneeling beside her box, my hands functioning as they were meant to, I watched the kittens uncurl, gasp and breathe, and was as happy as if I'd created them myself. That was when I found the answer to the why of my life.

Cleo was most generous in giving me happiness. Regularly she made the terrifying journey down the fire ladder to spend the night in the courtyard, until her progeny numbered fifteen. Our landlord didn't object. He could hardly, with all those dogs. The neighbors never complained; each had a fault of his own that made silence expedient. The superintendent was a jolly Negro who luckily had the same weakness as ours, a basement full of strays, one of them no doubt Cleo's aid in making me happy. But we ourselves were discommoded; too often having to choose between not working or brushing cats off the table to make room for the typewriters; remaining standing or lifting a heap of cats from a chair; lying in one position all night or upheaving a blanket that growled at us. Most of our friends stopped visiting, even though we kept a brush at the door to remove hairs from their clothing when they left.

In the Catskill Mountains we had a little house where we spent summers whenever we could afford to, and this seemed to offer a solution to our growing problem. There was no particular need for us to stay in the city; we could do our work anywhere. So we hired a truck, placed Cleo and our other charges inside, and drove off to live in the country. True, whenever it rained we were just as crowded as we had been in the apartment, but even in the Catskills rain does not fall every day.

While we were still living in the city, whenever I couldn't sleep at night, I used to go for a walk. I would start at the road where there was a good view of the mountains, fill my lungs with the crisp, clean air—always I chose a day that was slightly nippy, for this is proper climate in the mountains—and go up the winding path, past the aged hemlock leaning so far to the east you would have thought only a touch could bring it down, yet year after

5

year it stands against winter gales; past the little green house, to another tree.

In those days a great sugar maple towered over the house. You could look up and up and not see the top; you had to stand some distance away, and viewed from there, the house itself became irrelevant, like a small growth attached to the magnificent giant's roots. Woodsmen warned us: "If that tree ever comes down, your house will be a pile of matchsticks." Our neighbor down the road said, "It takes over a hundred years to grow a tree like that, and only fifteen minutes to cut it down." We let the maple stand.

Then came the hurricane. That summer I was staying in the house alone. Clad in raincoat and rubber boots for ready escape, should leaving my fragile shelter be necessary or, indeed, possible, I stood at the window viewing the holocaust beyond: great branches floating past like twigs, one tree after another keeling over in dream-like soundlessness under the screaming of the wind. The huge maple swayed toward me and away, toward me and away, the earth at its feet bulging and subsiding as the roots strained to keep their hold. In three hours I aged twice that number of years, and twisted all the buttons off the raincoat. In the city, Eric worried. As soon as the roads were passable he came to sentence the tree.

"You can't go through anything like that again. It will have to come down."

The woodsmen peered up and scratched their heads, prowled around, measuring, calculating, raising their arms to salute the monarch and draw lines along the ground.

"Might just barely make it," they said.

In the house I listened to the snick-snack of the saw, feeling the rasp in my own body. Fifteen minutes, our neighbor had said. I watched the hand of the clock creep toward destruction, waited for the loud crack, the rush of leaves past the window, the sickening rising jolt of the floor under my feet. Outside, the woodsmen were leaning on their axes, grinning. "Not an inch to spare," they said. Close against the house lay the immense bole; the branches, bunches of keys hanging limp, leaves fluttering in extremis, stretched far away, across the brook, into the woods beyond. I put my hand on the cool, moist, white flesh, stroked

6

it, saw the brown spot in the center, and was relieved. "There, you see?" I said. "It was beginning to rot." One of the woodsmen shook his head. "Oh, that ain't rot, ma'am," he said. "That's its heart." I went back into the house and wept.

So, on my walks, I went first to this tree, to put my arms around it, as far as they would reach, and lay my cheek against its rough bark. There were others I loved, but the maple I revered. Then, having paid homage, I went to the brook just in back of the house, at these times running just right, not thundering, nor hiding in furtive trickles under the rocks. At the pool I squatted, to watch water striders skip over the surface toward a moth floating death-spread, and as usual, dipped my hand under the moth to hold it, sodden, hoping the fragile wings would flutter back to life. On my night walks they always did.

Beyond the brook lay the woodlot, a stand of tall, straight hemlocks we kept meticulously clean, Eric on a ladder stripping away dead limbs, I gathering the debris onto a great pile in which wrens might nest. On my walks I sat here for a while, then went down the hill to our sunrock, a bulging boulder dropped eons ago by a melting glacier, where we used to lie covered by the blue sky on hot summer days; and on to the hidden pool, behind a screen of tall goldenrod parted by many animal paths, into which we plunged, gasping, to cool off.

This was where our land ended. I knew every rock along the lower border, and where woodchuck holes lay under leaves to trap unwary feet. At the far end I would come uphill again through a tangle of berry bushes and brush, to pause at the top beside a huge ant mound. Many hours I have watched over that busy edifice, trying to make some sense out of the many comings and goings. Ants are well-organized creatures, I've been told, but the one I watch finds a dead brother, with extreme difficulty lugs the corpse all the way up the mound, and having reached the summit, carries it back down again. Perhaps such a journey has meaning, but what that might be I have not yet discovered.

From the ant hill I returned to the path, went past the leaning hemlock once more, and this time, to the house. The door shouted welcome when I turned the knob, and inside was the good, clean smell of forest mold.

The house is somewhat larger and better equipped now. Then 7 it was only one room, with an appendage given more dignity than deserved when called a bedroom. We slept on bunks, drew water from the pool, and comfort from a sturdy but graceful little wood stove; Arabella was her name. I still grow wistful over that stove. It was replaced by a clumsy space heater when I discovered I could not keep Arabella adequately supplied, those long winter days I was away, traveling to the hospital and back. A wood fire sounds warm, making you feel warmer no matter what the temperature might be. On my night visits the fire in Arabella had just been built, kindling sputtered cheerfully, and an orange glow danced through her friendly eye to play over the walls and floor.

The next morning, if it happened to be winter, I told Eric, "I went for a walk last night." He knew what I meant. But in a summer of down-turned luck that forced us to remain in the city's swelter I said nothing, not wanting to add to the hurt of poverty. Nevertheless he was aware of my longing; on a hot night when neither of us could sleep, the silence of pretended sleep would be broken by his apology: "I'm sorry you can't get away this year."

Thus, when we hired the truck and drove toward the hills, my joy was his also. We hadn't the slightest idea of how we would get along, and to tell the truth we didn't very well, only just keeping even with the grocery bill, sometimes not even that; out of the city, we were also out of editors' minds. Whenever our financial chart took a real nosedive, as too often it did, the animals were fed just the same—how could they comprehend poverty?—and we bought pancake flour. Not being of a domestic turn, I am to this day quite confounded by a steak; but after years of practice, at least I can make pretty good pancakes.

Whether we enjoyed them or not, whether we'd have to stay on this diet for weeks or months, such considerations became irrelevant under the sun of a benign summer day. "Who wants to go for a walk?" we'd call. Bounding in from all directions the cats would foregather, the dog would be already at our heels, knowing we'd call, and together we'd go along the way I had taken so often alone, on those sleepless nights in the city.

That was the beginning. Later there were others in the entourage, a goat, a raccoon, and for a while, an opossum.

In those days of outside plumbing, we dipped water from the pool, carried it into the house by the pailful, heated it on the wood stove, bathed in a rubber tub that could be folded and stored in a closet. The other bathroom accessory was located partway down the hill in a tiny house which came to be known as the kitchenette. Whenever it rained, visits to this place required advance planning: donning raincoat, rainhat, and, in heavy downpours that flooded adjacent territory, rubber boots. In winter, preparations were even more elaborate, involving coat, cap, muffler, mittens, arctics, and the trip itself was venturesome, occasionally ending up in the horizontal. But on fine nights the visit was a welcome respite from duties, which I took advantage of possibly more often than absolutely necessary and prolonged beyond requirement, enjoying the feel of night close around me, listening to small mysterious footfalls and rustlings, gazing up at the stars winking through the treetops. I always had noble thoughts in the kitchenette.

All about were hemlocks that dipped graceful branches to caress the earth, and closed overhead to form a dome. I felt almost as if I were in a cathedral. To one side was a pile of twigs and sticks, a tepee-like structure that somewhat resembled a beaver house. Day after day we passed this mound, and not once did either of us wonder how it had got there, or what it was for, until one night I heard a small song issue from it. A bird, singing at night, inside a pile of brush? I trained my flashlight on the mound and at once the song stopped; I switched off the light, waited, and after a while heard it again, a soft cooing that was like the contented murmuring of a dove as it preened its feathers before retiring at the end of the day.

After that, I visited the kitchenette even more often and stayed longer, sitting part of the time in front of the mound, staring at the pathway of beaten earth that tunneled under it. On moonlit nights I could see well enough; on dark nights I used the torch, but turned away from the tunnel, so that bright light would not shine in. I put down a piece of bread and sat very still, not even scratching mosquito bites, saw nothing but often heard the song; and when I next went to the kitchenette, the bread was always gone.

Finally one night I caught just a glimpse of something: a rodent head and two dainty white feet. The fur was buff, the ears were large and erect, the expression in the black eyes was inquisitive and friendly.That much I had time to see before the animal withdrew.

Evidently this brief appearance was to test my good will; the next night she trusted me enough to come out and snatch the bread, and I saw she was heavy with young. There was nothing furtive or unpleasant or ugly about her. The buff coat was sleek and clean and she moved with some grace. But the long tail betrayed her. She was a rat.

A rat that sang and had dainty white feet; what kind could that be? I thumbed through animal books, finally found her, and was relieved to learn she was considered reputable, even, in some parts of our country, edible; a white-throated wood rat, or trade rat. I called her Mrs. R.

Instead of bread, sometimes I gave her oatmeal or a plate of food the cats had left. She did not trust me enough to eat while I watched, but later the food and also the plate would be gone. Where it had been, there was always a little pile of stones. About the same time, I missed the keys to my trunk and sewing machine, a paring knife, a small screwdriver, and found stones where I'd evidently left them. The wood rat has a compulsion to steal things but also a conscience, and leaves something in fair exchange; hence the alternative appellation, trade rat. Investigators have torn apart nests to find them packed with spoons, knives, forks, small tools, dishes, even shoes. I left Mrs. R's intact, although I sorely missed the keys.

One evening I walked under a tree, happened to glance up, and there was Mrs. R sitting on a branch just over my head. Without thinking I reached up to touch her. She stayed quite still, even when I stroked her back and belly. Later I discovered deer mice react in the same way; somehow height seems to make tree climbers lose their fear of humans.

Thereafter I often caught sight of Mrs. R among the branches of the hemlocks, quite high up. If frightened, she would run to the end of a limb, jump to catch hold of another lower down, and so reach the ground to scamper off to safety in her tepee. She could drop as much as ten feet without apparent injury.

A night came when she did not appear immediately after I had put down the food and called to her. Instead, on all sides of her dwelling, in various doorways I had not noticed before, a lot of little heads peeped out. She had had her family, evidently quite a large one, although baby heads came and went so rapidly that I could not make an accurate count. Smelling the food, they grew bold and clustered in the main entrance of the tepee, where they looked like a bunch of flowers. The smallest ventured forth, in little fits and starts, pausing often to sit up, pink nose twitching to search out danger, and came at last to the dish; he sampled the food, then took a crumb back to his timid companions, who one by one followed the trail he had broken for them, until many were circled around the feast. But suddenly there was a rustle off to one side, and Mrs. R bounded over to dive into the tepee. With a cry that for them must have been very loud but was hardly audible to me, she gave warning, and at once they were all gone, even the bold one. I peered into the tunnel, shining my light so that it lit up a good portion of the interior. The earth floor, packed hard by many small feet, was as smooth and clean as if it had been swept every day. Far back I caught sight of one delicate white foot, but only for an instant.

As if the owner knew it had become visible, it was hastily withdrawn.

Poor Mrs. R found it impossible to control her large family. On succeeding nights the babies came immediately when I put down the dish; she called and called, but they paid no attention. With the serene confidence of youth, they accepted me as a friend, and having done so, became overbold.

The first time I noticed, I was startled; then I took their company for granted. Wherever I went at night there was a light patter of feet behind me. All the baby rats, grown now and changed in color from the soft gray of infancy to the buff of adulthood, were in attendance, making me feel something like the Pied Piper of Hamelin. But no mountain opened before us, and I began to worry. Wood rats can have as many as three litters a year. If Mrs. R and the females in this litter all produced bumper crops, how many rats would eventually tag after me?

Nature took care of that problem. Soon I heard owls hooting in the neighborhood and the rats gradually disappeared, until only one was left. Perhaps it was the bold one, for he made an unorthodox exit from his shelter during the day and was promptly caught by Kate, one of our female cats.

There are exceptions to every rule, but usually well-fed male cats don't hunt much. In the female, however, regardless of need, there is an age-old instinct to provide meat for her young. Should there be no young, a favorite human usually becomes the recipient. So Kate, out of family at the moment, gave me the rat, very much alive and non the worse for his misadventure. I didn't know what to do with him; if I let him go, chances were he'd be foolish enough to challenge fate again, perhaps with less luck. In the end I decided to keep him, named him Mr. R and put him in a cage.

Of all the animals I have known, Mr. R was the cleanest, downright fussy, in fact. The floor of his cage was always immaculate, except the one corner used for sanitary purposes. He never spilled his milk or scattered his oatmeal, and every day he made his bed. As soon as I gave him fresh tissue he would remove the previous day's from his box, carry it to his dump—the sanitation corner—and when every last scrap was gone, put in the new bedding, which was carefully spread and tamped down with feet and nose. This was not very much for him to do in the long day, and he must have missed his life of peril and adventure, scuttling over the earth and among the branches, just one step ahead of annihilation. He lived for only a year and, I suspect, died of boredom.

Meanwhile Mrs. R, having retained her mistrust of all things, including me, lived on to produce more young, and most of these, not exposed to my meddling and thus as cautious as their mother, survived also. This was the first installment of a lesson that I have been a long time learning: making friends with wild animals causes them to relax vigilance and may well cost them their lives.

Now, if I see a deer, I throw stones at it. I clap my hands to frighten chipmunks, squirrels, even birds. I will not act as procurer for the hunter with his rifle, the small boy with his slingshot or air gun, nor for any other predator prowling the woods and fields.

In childhood I was somewhat sickly and had few human play-
mates, but there was a dog friend, a mongrel tramp that
preferred to be free of commitments and had no home in particular. Perhaps ours was most favored; whenever he became too
lean or fly-bitten, he always paid us a visit. Shouting, "Curly's
here! Curly's here!" I would run into the house, my mother
would search the icebox or open a can, and once this first need
had been taken care of, we would put salve on his bleeding ears.
Sometimes he stayed with us only a day or two, sometimes a week
or more. By the hour I squatted beside him, running fingers
through his kinky fur, demanding no response from him, made
happy only by his presence. Then he would be off again, but
even while he was gone I was not unhappy; there was his next
visit to anticipate.

He had not been to see us in some time when a neighbor came
to tell us the policeman had him tied up in the vacant lot at the
corner. Curly had not bitten anyone or done anything bad, but
had been reported by some misanthrope as a vagrant, and in
those days the policeman on duty took care of such complaints,
on the spot, with his revolver. We bolted out of the house, my

mother and I, and while we were running we heard the shot; by the time we reached the corner the crowd that had gathered was already dispersing. My mother wouldn't let me look, turned me around, and led me back home; so even though I knew Curly was dead, I could not believe in his dying, and kept looking for him to come back again.

That was my first dog, if you could call him mine, and for years there was no other, not until I was grown and spending summers, or as much of them as we could afford, in the Catskills. Judy wasn't really my dog either. A wiggly little white mutt who curled her lips in a ferocious grin if she liked you and hid under the house if she didn't, she belonged to two boys who lived some distance down the road, the fore part to the elder, the hind to the younger, with all duties pertaining to her thus precisely allocated. In my opinion the owner of the rear, considered less fortunate, had the better of the bargain; although less attractive, this end demanded no service once Judy had been housebroken. The mouth continued to require regular feeding. However, as soon as I arrived, the whole dog moved out of their house and into mine.

If I planned to stay the entire summer, this arrangement was satisfactory to everyone; the boys were entirely free to enjoy vacation, I enjoyed Judy's company, and Judy herself was ecstatic. For about a week she trotted happily down and up the road, relocating her large collection of bones. Then, once the last of them had been disinterred, transported and reinterred, she was free to devote all her bounding attention to me; we wandered through the woods together, shared my dinner and my bed, she burrowed under the covers at my feet. Whenever her true owners paid a visit, she greeted them graciously but remotely, secure in her belief that she was for all time where she wanted most to be.

When I had money for only a short stay I was distressed, and so were the boys. One year I did not get to the mountains until late in the fall, and then only for a two-week visit, a small windfall having made this possible. Most of those two weeks Judy was on the road, carrying bones dug out of ground already hardened with frost at one end, to bury them in equally inhospitable soil at the other. When the work was at last finished and she could rest at my feet, suddenly I was gone again, and she had all the moving to do over.

Sometimes she would not go home. The boys would wait a while, then walk up the road, to find her sitting on the steps of the deserted house or huddled in a bed of leaves beside it. How was she to know I would not be back in an hour or a day, perhaps not for months or a year?

In the end I betrayed her, but that had to be. She was a lucky dog with a good home and a loving family. She didn't really need me. Muff did.

It was one of those summers, like many others, in which there was only money enough to send me and some of the cats to the country. Eric stayed in the city, writing copious long letters and sweltering, taking care of the cats that had been left behind. I had been settled only a short time, Judy was still busy moving, and had just gone off for another bone when I happened to wander out to the road, and saw in the middle of it a drooping black bundle that looked as if it had been everywhere, gone through everything, and quite run out of energy for further adventure; the next car would surely run it down. I called out, the bundle rolled the whites of its eyes, showed a red tongue and crept over to sit on my foot. "Good dog," I murmured, pulling out my foot and walking away. The bundle followed. "Go home now," I said, and went back to trimming dead branches from the hemlocks in front of the house. The bundle lay on the ground nearby and gazed at me soulfully. I turned my back; if ignored, it would leave, I thought.

Brush was thick and tall around the hemlocks; Judy, coming toward me wagging her tail, a bone in her mouth, did not see the bundle until it stood to get a better look at her. Possibly she thought I had acquired a bear; she gave one smothered yelp, dropped the bone, yelped again and went streaking down the road never to return, not even to claim her buried treasures.

I didn't want a dog, couldn't have a dog, I told the bundle. A city apartment was no proper place for a dog, at least not for one brought up in the country. Besides, there were the cats to think of; they had adjusted to Judy, but would they to another dog that also might look to them more like a bear? No, definitely, I didn't want a dog.

The bundle grinned in apparent agreement, sat down to sweep the ground with a plumy tail, yawned and rested head on paws, but the eyes did not close; they stared at me resolutely, until at last I gave in. "I suppose you're hungry," I said.

I would not let her into the house but gave her a bowl of bread and milk and some scraps of meat at the foot of the steps. Then, after she had gulped down everything and had a drink of water, I capitulated further. Already light was gone from the woods, soon it would be night, and I hated to think of anything being homeless in the dark. "All right," I said, "you can stay overnight. Tomorrow we'll find out where you belong, or where you might belong."

She was cautious and canny in her determination to please. Straight through the house she marched looking neither to the right nor the left, past the cats' glare, into the clothes closet where I had put down a quilt. There she stayed the whole night, without a whimper or even a rustle.

The next day did not turn up a home for her, but inquiry told me much about her. She had stayed with the butcher for a while, and the laundryman, and the milkman, but had left even though they showed her every courtesy. She had been pursued and almost shot by the dog warden. At various other doors she had begged handouts and always found welcome, for she was a handsome dog, a water spaniel of good breeding. Only when she came to me, the sole human among those she had encountered who didn't want her, did she choose to remain.

When night came once again I told her she might stay until morning, but then she'd really have to go—somewhere. Again she marched obediently into the closet and lay down on the quilt with a determination to please and possess that surely would have won me over if I had not been equally determined not to possess.

The following day, cows belonging to a farmer some distance up the road broke out of their pasture again and, as always, headed straight for my straggly but beloved flower garden. Since they passed acceptable grazing all along their route without pausing even to sniff, I could only conclude they congregated in the garden to plague me. As usual, I gave a puny shout that was ignored, and while they nibbled delicately on petunias, ran indoors to fetch the broom. Even this was not too effective, but after persistent poking and prodding and swatting, they would eventually wander off. On this day, however, I didn't need the broom. Alerted by my shout, my unwelcome dog went charging at them, rounded them up nicely and drove them off.

I praised her, and sat on the steps with my hand on her head to think. "You are a useful dog," I finally concluded. "If you like, you can stay here the rest of the summer. When I leave for the city we'll find another home for you."

Named Muff because she was so like one in appearance, round and wooly, she was in truth anything but a cuddly dog, a pet to be pampered. Her desire was to be useful; her job was to take care of me and whatever I valued. My likes and dislikes, peculiar though they might seem, were hers also. Therefore, toward the cats, other dogs I favored, and later, goats, raccoons, chipmunks, even mice, she was benignly protective; toward those I disfavored, like the cows, she was never vicious, only aloof, annoyed or angry, depending upon the degree and quality of my reaction.

That is not to say she was just a mirror. In matters pertaining to my welfare, she had a will of her own. I was a most exasperating charge; going over rough ground, I paid no attention to where I put my feet and consequently fell down a lot. The fact that I never hurt myself, thanks to the invaluable training I had received, did not lessen her annoyance. Evidently in her opinion there always could be a first time. So she would fuss over me as I lay laughing, slapping my cheek with an anxious, impatient tongue, refusing to believe I was all right until I got up and showed her I could walk without even limping.

Once, going downhill, I slid on some loose stones, my legs shot out from under, and I sat down hard. This time she grunted with obvious disgust, as if she were saying, "Oh, no, not again!" As usual I was unhurt, and by the next day had forgotten all about the tumble. But she hadn't. When I started down the same hill she darted in front of me to place her body in the way, and when I moved to circle around her she moved also, making it clear that I'd have to detour. For two weeks thereafter I was under suspicion, then was allowed to make a trial run of the hill, during which I stayed entirely upright, causing her to dance with approval.

Another afternoon, she was outside sunning herself on the steps while I cleaned the house, when suddenly a shelf on which a lot of bottles were stored came crashing down. She must have thought I had at last taken a really critical fall and came plunging into the house, making a frightful racket of her own as she knocked things down in her haste. The combination of worry and downright disgust in her eyes was so funny that I had to laugh, and such a display of flippancy over what she considered a matter of the utmost gravity infuriated her so that she stalked off in a huff, only to return almost immediately to tell me how relieved she was.

All through the summer she stayed close by my side, not even lured away by a seductive male dog or a yapping pack on a hunt in the woods. When I went shopping she trotted at my heels. In the store she lay near the door, her eyes following me around, even in such surroundings with a touch of apprehension, always on guard against disaster.

She also accompanied me on my rambles through the woods, which more often than not involved hours and miles, although my intention at the start had been otherwise. Some people have a sense of direction; they seem to know always which way they are going and how to get back by the same route. I am not so blessed. Out of sight of the house, even on our own land, I am at once lost and may wander for an unconscionably long time, evidently in circles although I am sure my course is straight as the crow's, until some accidental deviation from orbit happens to cross familiar territory. I tried placing mounds of stones on rocks and breaking twigs, but somehow missed even these markers. Often, therefore, I would spend a whole day in the woods simply because I didn't know how to get out.

Usually the cats started out with me, after a number of rounds grew tired, and went off on their own. Now, with unquestioning patience, Muff accompanied me the whole of the way, casting a sidelong glance every once in a while, probably when we came quite close to the house and turned away, but otherwise showing no doubt as to my wisdom. Then came a day when we must have walked in a straight line for a while, so that once we finally started circling, we were entirely too far away from home to bump into it. After a few hours of steady plodding Muff began to show some reluctance to go on, but I was not particularly worried, having been lucky up to then, until we entered an ancient, dense pine forest, so unlike the rest of the woods, that I knew I had never been there before. At the same time I noticed it had become difficult to pick my way over the springy carpet of needles that lay in deep shadow under the trees, and with a touch of panic realized the sun had set. Evidently this time we were really lost. I tripped over a root and Muff gave me an anxious look.

"Well," I said to her with jolly optimism, to conceal my uneasiness, "we'd better be getting home." Her tail went up, the anxious expression changed to one of approval, and with a bound she was off in one direction even as I turned to go in another. "No, this way, Muff," I said, although I should have known better. Her tail curled between her legs but she followed me, and with infallible error I led her to a swamp, where bright green moss glistened wetly in the failing light and belched obscenely under our feet. Mine were soaked immediately. Muff tried to pick her way with care, hopping from jutting rock to hillock, but after missing a few times gave up and squelched dejectedly behind me.

Approaching darkness had cooled the air. With no sweater, and water sloshing in my shoes, I was quite as miserable as Muff, but managed to keep up a pretense of assurance until we came to the cliff. It was high and sheer, and trying to scale it seemed not only foolhardy but pointless. At least I knew our house was not perched on a precipice. Sitting on a damp boulder I gazed at the unpleasant prospect of spending the night in the woods and, if we were lucky, being subjected to the embarrassment of rescue by a searching party the following day. Muff squatted beside me, leaning against me, and stared dolefully at our oozing footprints in the moss.

"Trouble is," I said, an omnicient admitting ignorance, "I don't know where home is."

At once she was off the rock and away at a brisk trot, paws slapping carelessly through the muck, head high, tail waving. Pausing, she glanced back over her shoulder, and her eyes said, "Well, are you coming?"

I was sure she was wrong, but since I had no idea what was right, I followed her. Somehow we got out of the swamp almost immediately and by-passed the pine forest. Soon, to my relief, a clearing came in sight, and the vague outline of a house. Imagine, I thought, someone living this far back in the woods. I wondered who it might be. Then the house took on a familiar aspect; it was our own. Without once having touched her nose to the ground to pick up a scent, Muff had taken me by short cut straight home.

For weeks after this adventure I prowled through the woods in every direction, trying to find again the pine forest, the swamp, and the cliff; I never did, and finally came to suspect they were indeed, as Eric said in a delightful malapropism, "a filament of my imagination." But now I wandered without a care, knowing that no matter which way I went, or how far, the magic words "Muff, take me home" would whisk me there.

Once we somehow got inside a pasture and came face to face with a bull. The bull charged, but so did Muff, and with some of the fanciest footwork I'd ever seen kept the big beast at bay until I had climbed over the fence. Then, while I held my breath, she ducked under.

It was perfectly wonderful to have a dog. How had I lived, how could I live without one?

The nights turned cold, leaves whispered down from the trees, and I invented various excuses in reply to Eric's increasingly impatient queries as to when I was coming "home." Muff and I romped through wind-driven dunes of crisp dead leaves, and almost every day, somewhere she found a gift for me. At first I was puzzled, for she barred my path much as she had the time I was not allowed to go over the loose stones; here I was sure I had never fallen. I tried to pass her, but she began to weave at my feet in a most peculiar way, making me fear she might be ill, until I noticed she had something in her mouth. At once, seeming to sense I comprehended at last, she put down the small burden, a dead bird. So gently had she carried it that not a feather was out of place.

I thanked her and buried the bird. She dug it up and gave it to me again. There was nothing else to do; I took it home and after much searching, found a hollow tree in which the bird might be placed out of her reach. Of this disposal she approved.

Never did she harm anything, not even a bedroom slipper, but her knack for finding cadavers, mostly of ripe age, soon filled 21 the tree hollow, which came to be known as her treasure chest, and I had to locate another. Shrews, chipmunks, mice, the skin of a snake, a dried-up frog, or only a small piece of unidentifiable pelt—whatever it was, she carried it carefully and proudly, her head high; eventually I came to know by her manner of walking that I was to receive another gift.

The only time we had a difference of opinion was when she retrieved an entire pig's head, remnant of our neighbor's slaughtering, which she dragged home with great difficulty and gave to me with particular pride. No tree hollow anywhere was big enough to accomodate this, so I locked her in the house and took a walk without her, to hide the pig's head in a clump of bushes. She found it in no time and dragged it back. I buried it; she dug it up. Finally I paid a passing boy fifty cents to tote it about a mile away on his bicycle.

The first snow fell, and Eric's letters became insistent. I had to confess. "I have adopted a dog," I wrote. "I can't give her up." His letter in reply didn't say, "How can we keep her in this small apartment? How can we feed her when things get rough? Who will care for her, take her for walks? Don't we have enough, with all the cats?" No, it contained none of the objections I had anticipated. All it said was, "You know I like dogs."

Evidently there was much I didn't know; I needn't have had any qualms either about Muff adjusting to city life. Wherever I was, that was home to her, and the streets of New York were not too different from country roads as long as we walked them together. She still had duties. One was to protect me from yawning subway entrances, around which she forced me to make wide detours. Another, to go down with Eric each morning to the mail box, where he stuffed into her mouth whatever letters there were and sent her back up the two flights, with nothing ever lost, not even a bill. Still another was to keep order among the cats. At the first hint of bickering she stepped in, like a policeman settling a street brawl, to separate the combatants, and send them off in different directions with an authoritative snort.

She was not one to play favorites. Although I was boss, primarily because enforcing discipline was an unpleasant task Eric left to me, she gave us equal love, and her supreme pleasure was to go walking with the two of us, trotting head high, as if saying to all we met, "These are mine!" One afternoon Eric had to go uptown, and since it was time for Muff's stroll, said he'd accompany us as far as the subway station. Neither of us gave a thought to Muff's fear of these portals of hell.

We reached the corner. "Goodbye, Muff," Eric said, giving her a pat; then, while she strained at the leash, desperately trying to head him off, he went straight into the terrible hole. Whimpering, she circled around, sat down, got up, sat down again; crouching low, she edged closer to stare into the hole, paying no attention to all the people brushing past. "Come, Muff," I begged, but she would not. "Your master is all right," I told her. "Muff, he's home." She wouldn't believe me. I tried to pull her and she slid along the pavement, eyes still on the subway entrance; I had to stop and she lay down, head between her paws. Passers-by paused to ask solicitously, "Is your dog sick?" and how could I explain? A small crowd collected. Embarrassed, I finally picked her up and carried her home, no easy task; she weighed nearly forty-five pounds and hung like a dead weight.

Back in the apartment she put herself in a corner, faced the wall to grieve, and there she stayed until Eric's step on the stairs touched off an explosion of joy. That experience taught us a lesson. Never again did the three of us start out together unless we would return together.

In the mountains Muff had gone free, but the laws of the city required a leash; to accustom her to this restraint she was given a lesson each afternoon, just before she had her dinner. Three times she traveled with me around the apartment, close by my side; whenever I stopped, she had to also, and when I went on, she was to keep smartly at my heels. So swiftly did she learn that in a few days further lessons seemed unnecessary, but without them she moped and would not eat her dinner. This also had become a duty, and she loved duties. So, to please her and add variety, I thought up more difficult lessons.

We paced out figure eights, walked together backwards; she learned to "sit" and "stay," to come at once and stand beside me when I called. This last lesson saved us from a fine one day when we were strolling on the river front. With no other dogs or people in sight, I had slipped off her leash to let her run. Suddenly a patrol car swept around a corner and stopped, the door 23 opened and a policeman got out, notebook in hand, his eyes traveling from Muff to me. She was some distance ahead, playing, but turned at once when I called "Heel," and came to stand beside me like a soldier. The officer grinned and crawled back into the car.

Again, I was glad she was trained when we found Matilda.

We were near Gramercy Park one cold, blustery, dismal day when we saw a pigeon, huddled against the wall of a building, heavy shoes and spiked heels passing close, threatening death or maiming any instant. I too might have gone by without noticing, if Muff hadn't urged me across the pavement and stood over the little thing. All of her body stiffly immobile, except for the tail that waved, she looked up to me for instructions. "Shoo!" I said to the pigeon; it shuffled a bit, and I saw it had an injured leg. A doorman came strolling over. "Been there for hours," he said. "Can't fly. Baby, I guess." What would happen to it? He shrugged his shoulders. "Somebody'll finally step on it, I suppose. Or a cat will come along."

I scooped up the pigeon. Muff and I changed course; heads down against the wind, we went to the spca, some distance away near the river. The man on duty there examined the pigeon. "Squab," he said. "Young one." He laughed and added, "Make good eating." As for giving it shelter, they had no accomodations for birds.

The pigeon snuggled down in my hand, glad to be back; Muff and I started for home, and at the first hardware store we came to I bought wire. It cost three dollars. That I remember very well, for three dollars was all I had, and I was supposed to spend it on groceries. "Your master will be furious," I told Muff, although I knew better. He'd look at the bird and say, "Yes, but . . ." and sit down to canned beans as if that was what he had expected anyway.

That evening I made the first of the many, many cages I have built. Inside it, the pigeon picked at bread and waltzed on one leg, earning the name Matilda. "Yes, but . . ." Eric said, "What will you do with her?"

"Teach her to fly," I answered.

Once each day the cats were locked in the bathroom and Muff was placed in a corner to sit-stay. Matilda was already fluttering, having learned that these steps preceded release. As soon as I opened the cage she was on my hand, crooning; she loved my hand, and me. Clinging to a finger, one foot at an awkward angle, she rode to the far wall, and in her corner Muff danced up and down with excitement. "Now, Matilda, fly!" I threw her in the air, she beat her wings and plummeted to sprawl on the floor, I picked her up, threw her again. Day after day she fell, and fell; then she did not come down so hard or so soon, and at last she was flying, back and forth, lighting on the valance and returning to rest on my shoulder. She would have been content to stay there, but grew restive in the cage. It was time for her to be free. So on a day when the sun shone and the air was balmy, Muff and Matilda and I went for a walk, to Madison Square Park, where there were other pigeons, and every day, winter or summer, good people who came with sacks of bread or seeds or nuts. Huddled on my shoulder, Matilda looked at this strange world with fear. But on the avenue a horn blew, startling her so that she took off for a nearby tree, and Muff and I hurried away.

I did not know then how difficult it is for any animal raised in captivity to adjust to freedom, nor how hostile others can be toward a stranger. After Matilda's release, Muff and I strolled through the park each day, looking for a bird with a crooked foot, but never again did we see her. Perhaps we had merely put off her death by a few months; but at least in those months she had been given a certain small happiness and, in return, had given us something, a lesson in tolerance. Streets can be cleaned; that is what street cleaners are for. Life destroyed cannot be recalled. True, pigeons have alimentary tracts and eliminate as do people, although with less foul pollution of our earth and streams. True, they may transmit disease. But so may all other animals, including people. Glancing at the day's headlines, I dare to imagine how much nicer the world would be if pigeons remained, and humans were exterminated.

Muff was very unhappy. Each afternoon she went to sit in her corner, as if in doing so she could bring back Matilda. To divert her, I thought up more complicated lessons. Placing her dinner on the floor, I held her away saying, "Don't touch," over and over. Once she had learned the command she would sit near the dish, staring at it, not touching, until the words "Go   25

catch!" released her. Next came, "Don't touch, come away."
This was hard for her and almost heartbreaking for me, she
wilted so with sadness, but dutifully she turned and walked away
from her dinner.

Actually, such training had purpose. Whenever I wasn't looking, she gobbled up whatever food was left on the cats' plate,
which put too much weight on her and displeased the cats. After
a few weeks of drilling I could put down the cats' food, say,
"Don't touch; come away; belongs to kitties"—a word she comprehended more readily than "cat"—then leave the room knowing that no matter how long I was gone, she would not eat the
food. There was one small compromise. Whatever crumbs
slipped off the plate she considered fair findings. Her black nose
would go snuffling along sweeping the floor, sometimes even
nudging the plate aside to get at something that lay under its
rim, but never succumbing to the temptation of straying toward
the main feast.

Later she did think up a way to outwit her stern conscience
and appropriate the food without disobeying orders. "As long
as the plate is in the cat's corner," she must have reasoned, "the
food on it belongs to them. But if the whole plate is moved . . .?"
So, after having cleaned the floor, she took the plate between her
teeth, carried it across the room, placed it in her corner, and
licked it clean. Anything as cleverly thought out as that I hadn't
the heart to forbid; at least she waited politely until the cats had
quite finished eating.

She enjoyed life in the city and would have been content to
stay there for the rest of her days; but when we all spilled out of
the truck and her nostrils caught the old familiar scents of the
woods, she was delirious with joy. Now she had her proper jobs
back, protecting the cats from foxes and other dogs and strange
toms, chasing cows, making sure I didn't fall or get lost. And as
we acquired other animals, there was still more for her to do,
keeping the goats out of the garden, the raccoon off the table,
telling me exactly where the chipmunks were when they escaped
from the cage.

Sitting with her on the steps in the warm sunlight, her body
leaning against mine, my hand on her tousled head, I saw the
way her hair was graying and contemplated, dreaded life with-

out her. A milky film came into her eyes, those mirrors of my moods that were sympathetically reproachful when I sorrowed and danced with joy when I laughed; gradually the film thickened, until only white showed where there had been depth to read her thoughts. Then it was time for more lessons.

Up, Muff. Down, Muff. She acquired a vocabulary of nearly a hundred words, more than she needed to find her way through the dark. Left, Muff. Right, Muff. There is a kitty, don't bump into her. Here is a dog. Good dog, one of your friends. Say hello. Watch out! Stand still. Come, I'll lead you around the tree . . .

She obeyed with precision, as always, and at my command, would stop with one paw already lifted for the next step. She was much cleverer than I. I had only four words to learn, and could not; easy words: Goodbye, Muff, sleep well.

She lay at my feet, breathing slowly and more slowly, and then she was not breathing any more. That was how she left us. I called Eric, he knelt beside her, put his hand on the still body, stroked the rumpled fur, and suddenly doubled over. It was the only time I ever saw him cry, except one other, shortly before I found him dead, the gun fallen from his hand.

For a long while I could not walk in the woods. Wherever I went I was lopsided. We talked it over and I said no, I didn't want another dog, to overlay memories of her with others.

No, I don't want another dog; not unless one wants me, as much as she did, long ago.

Most people praise a cat for catching a mouse, but are indignant when the kill is a bird. Like the cat, I cannot make this fine distinction. To me (unlike the cat) both happenings are distressing, perhaps because I esteem mice as well as birds. However, this theory does not hold when applied to the shrew, a quarrelsome, gluttonous savage that is far from endearing; even so I hold it in my hand with some sorrow for its demise. The fact is I cannot abide any killing, whether by the soldier on the battlefield, the hunter in the forest, or the cat in the garden.

Often I have chased after a cat of mine, uphill, downhill, in and out of brush, to discover what was in its mouth—most often the lowly shrew, inedible, but being warm and soft, somewhat more fun to play with than a paper ball. Having appropriated the catch, I do not punish the captor, not even when the prey turns out to be the much loved thrush. Instead, we return to the house, and in exchange for what I have taken I give a piece of meat. Not being covered with fur or feathers, this is preferred food, and in time the cat, eager to receive the reward, delivers to me immediately, without stopping to kill. I am given a bird, hold it in my hand for a moment, then open the hand and watch it fly away. Disposal of live wingless donations, however, is not that easy. The canny cat, observing the release, will try to make the catch all over again, to earn still more meat. That was why, for a while, I gave lodging to so many chipmunks.

The first two, acquired almost simultaneously, were Napper and Bricks, the latter so named because the first day, while I put together a cage, she was housed in a cardboard box labeled "No. 465 Bricks." What kind of bricks they might have been was something I puzzled over briefly.

In those early days I didn't know that chipmunks would not live together amicably. Just to disprove the rule, these two did, sharing food and bed, at first nothing more than a heap of tissue on the floor of the cage, and working as a team to execute their many escapes. The cage had a small crack over the door, not big enough for anything but a worm to pass through, I thought, but somehow the chipmunks got out, apparently by osmosis. I rebuilt the cage, giving it a tighter door. The chipmunks cased this new door and discovered it was locked with hooks. Thrusting their paws through the wire mesh, one fiddled with the top hook, the other with the bottom; soon both hooks were pushed up and the door open. I substituted hasps and bolts; they had the bolts out in no time. I tried large safety pins, and one chipmunk must have said to the other, "Elementary, my dear Watson." I had hardly turned my back before they had snapped open and removed the pins. Finally I produced a complicated lock that involved lengths of wire and washers that slid over the wire to fasten the door. After days and days of concentrated study and repeated endeavor, the chipmunks gave up trying to solve this puzzle, which sometimes baffled me also.

I like to give captive animals at least an approximation of the life they led when free. Chipmunks, I had learned, lived in burrows under rocks or roots of trees or, if they were shiftless, lazy, "tobacco road" members of the species, in crevices in stone walls or people's cellars. A properly enterprising chipmunk might have a veritable underground castle of many rooms; bed, storage, and bath. This castle, in keeping with its elegance, had to have several entrances, front, side, and service, so to speak. Once, trying to photograph a chipmunk in the wild, I was puzzled when she took the nut I offered and skittered with it around and around my feet. After quite a while that must have greatly annoyed her, I discovered my foot was planted over her service entrance, through which the nut had to be taken, use of the front door for this purpose being highly improper.

To make Bricks and Napper feel at home, I spent much time and effort putting together wooden boxes that you could say were something like burrows. They chewed them up faster than I made them. I tried glass jars, which were indestructible, but eventually discarded because they tended to sweat. I bought sheet metal to make more boxes; they rusted and were difficult to clean. Finally our neighbor donated his empty tobacco tins, and the housing problem was solved. With small holes cut in for doorways, the cans were snug and dry, and I had only to remove the covers to clean them.

In one the chipmunks put their bedding, in the other, their nuts, thus duplicating their life in the wild. By apparent agreement one corner of the cage became their bathroom, and no other spot was ever used, although in the very beginning their water dish had been favored. This use of water is a trait shared by quite a few animals, and I've often wondered whether it might not have given inspiration for our modern plumbing. The skunk, raccoon, opossum, even the wood rat will squat on a rock close to the edge of a stream, so that their deposits will be washed away by high water after the next rain.

I had to clean out the chipmunks' houses, not because they were ever dirtied but because they got too full. Of all animals, these little ground squirrels are the most provident; even an empty stomach must stay that way while the larder is stocked. Bricks and Napper begged for nuts and more nuts, stuffed them in their storehouse until it overflowed, then put them in their sleeping quarters until there was no room left for sleeping and they had to spend the night curled up in a corner. At this stage I emptied the storehouse; over and over I gave them the same nuts, which didn't seem to bother them at all.

Usually I made my raids at night, when they were asleep; chipmunks have strong jaws and razor sharp teeth, and tend to resent intrusion, even by the hand that feeds them. Once, after I had emptied the storehouse and put it back, suspicion or an

untimely hunger woke Bricks. She went to what had been an

overstocked larder, stood for a moment in the doorway of the empty can transfixed with disbelief, screamed and scuttled back to wake Napper.

Together they went to confirm their loss, he somewhat groggily, his eyes only half open; they inspected the can, came out, looked around, went in again and began to argue, quietly at first, then more and more heatedly, until they were trading curses and blows. Probably each accused the other of thievery.

The next morning they were friendly again, but kept a wary eye on each other. Whenever one went into the storehouse, where a few nuts now rattled, the other followed to make sure the visit was legitimate.

Then one of the cats gave me another chipmunk, Pete, and with him, discord entered the cage. Bricks and Napper were fussy to a fault about keeping things neat; perhaps their resentment of Pete had something to do with his tendency to store perishables, like cherries or chunks of apple. They would throw out such moldering refuse, carefully sort their nuts, discarding all those that were not quite clean, and once they had the storehouse in immaculate order again, there would be Pete bringing in another sticky mess. But most likely he would have been unacceptable anyway. Bricks and Napper were the only chipmunks I ever put together that did not try to kill each other.

The seriousness of the disagreement was not apparent to me until one day, while I watched them pursue each other in what I thought was a game, I saw Pete go in one direction and his tail float off in another. Immediately I took him out, and built a separate apartment on top of the cage, where from then on he lived in solitary and sloppy contentment. To make up for the loss of his tail, which he didn't seem to miss, I gave him the biggest nuts, the first of the red raspberries and cream from the top of the bottle. And because he was such a garbage collector, I cleaned out his house oftener than the others'.

Of all the food I offered, milk was most favored. Napper, making his initial acquaintance with this delicacy, picked up the bowl to hold it between his paws while he drank, then must have had an idea that what was on the bottom might be even better than the top, turned the container over and spilled milk all down his shirt front. Visibly distressed, he tossed the dish away, washed himself desperately until he was clean again, and finally put himself sternly to bed.

Following Pete, more chipmunks arrived with rapidity, all but one donated by the cats, until the cage, having a new apartment tacked on to it for each new tenant, looked like a miniature skyscraper. Mr. Perkins was the last to come, late in the fall; he simply walked through the door one day, and when I put a box on the floor, hopped into it willingly. Evidently attracted by the contented chirping of the other residents, he must have decided he wanted to spend the winter in an apartment house also.

There was this proof that life in captivity was preferable; nevertheless it seemed a pity that such inquisitive, spirited animals should have no diversion from a dull routine of eating, sleeping, storing nuts, and quarreling with neighbors. I thought of giving them the freedom of the porch during the night, when all the cats had been brought into the house, then somehow persuading them to return to their proper quarters in the morning, before we let the cats out. We tried it, and the result was bedlam. All night long chipmunks cursed and fought, rattled up and down the screens pursuing and fleeing, filched nuts from each other and had them filched back again. The cats, roused from slumber by the racket, scratched at the door and whimpered to get out. We tried to shush the cats and nobody got any sleep. The next morning I spent over an hour rounding up and sorting out the chipmunks; Mr. Perkins had only half a tail; Becky had lost a toe; Nix, two toes; all looked thoroughly beaten up.

Next we tried letting them out one at a time, each being given a night of freedom in turn, and that worked out quite well, except for Bricks. She was caught in a crevice, and efforts to get her out dislodged a beam that killed her. Most of the others were good about returning to their homes, Napper the best of the lot. As soon as I called, he would come out of some hiding place to leap on my shoulder for a ride to the cage; then he would run down my arm and in. Pete was amiable enough, but stupid. When the door to the house was accidentally left open on his free morning, he dashed in, found a small hole on the underside of the sofa and squeezed himself in among the springs. There he stayed for several days, while the sofa bore a big sign saying,

DON'T SIT HERE. Finally, just as we were considering the advisability of tearing apart the sofa, thirst and hunger drove him out.

Becky was a tease; she would skip to her apartment door, almost enter, then with a mocking chortle flick up on my shoulder and go bounding across the porch. When I was in a hurry one morning she was particularly coquettish, darting here and there with her cheeks crammed full of Indian nuts, so that every time she moved, she rattled. Chipmunks can flit like fireflies, but as she whisked past I managed to grab her by the scruff of the neck, startling her so that she squawked, and all the Indian nuts spewed out of her mouth like buckshot. She was furious, but perhaps forgave me later when I picked up every Indian nut I could find and gave them back to her.

Every once in a while the chipmunks would houseclean, taking everything out of their cans and throwing whatever they wanted to get rid of on their feeding trays, which they had learned would be removed each day; the rest was stuffed into their mouths and carried back in. For a while I was busy and neglected to empty their storehouses. All of them became selective and placed on their trays nuts they didn't particularly like; all but Napper. He couldn't part with any of his, and finally had his sleeping can so stuffed that he could hardly get in, and having done so with difficulty, found it impossible to sleep on such a bumpy bed. All night long he'd rattle around among the nuts, trying to find a comfortable spot.

At last he evidently decided some of the nuts would simply have to go. Everything was removed from his house. The bedding was put to one side, the nuts placed all around the edge of the feeding tray, neatly lined up and carefully sorted as to size. Then he appeared to do some serious thinking. He went along the row of nuts, examining, nudging with his nose those that had rolled slightly out of line, went into his empty house, came out and stared at the nuts again. Finally he carried them all back in, threw his bedding on top any old way and spent another sleepless night. The next day I took pity on him; as soon as I emptied his storehouse he gratefully transferred to it all the lumps in his mattress, made his bed properly, then slept and slept.

Each chipmunk had a unique personality. Midge loved people, and always danced for visitors, sommersaults being her specialty. She also loved to tease the cats. Living in the penthouse, she would entice them to the top of the cage, then run upside down underneath them to nip their paws. Whenever I heard a cat yelp on the porch, I knew she had tricked one again.

Pete never made friends with anyone but me. Becky, the tease, almost preferred biting a finger to taking the proffered nut. Mr. Perkins was gravely dignified; Gramps, an old fellow who wanted only to finish his life in peace. Nix, true to her name, didn't particularly like anybody or anything, not even, I sometimes suspected, herself; Napper was just the opposite. He seemed to have true chipmunk-sized affection for me, liked to sit on my shoulder and would touch my cheek gently with his nose or tiny paw. And he was the only one who built a fortress.

When the air grew cold with coming winter, the other chipmunks stayed most of the time in their houses, sleeping or rustling around, tamping down tissue to make their beds more comfortable. Napper remained active outside, making odd little wads from the tissue I gave him, and also the newspaper that lined his tray. These he pasted on the wire of the cage. What made them stick I don't know; there must have been some ingredient in his saliva that acted like glue. By the time the first snow fell he had insulated the whole of his apartment with a thick wall of paper, except for the door, which he left untouched.

Chipmunks are seldom seen during winter, but don't truly hibernate. Sometimes I hear one chirping under the snow, and a clever fellow who lived near our house one year made a long curved tunnel through the snow, from his dwelling to the bird feeding station, a constant source of food. Every morning red squirrels plugged up the entrance to his tunnel, and every day he dug it out again, unless I took pity on him and removed the snow block myself.

In their comfortable, well-stocked apartments, our chipmunks slept most of the time, but came out briefly each day to pick up fresh tissue and nuts, drink their milk and perhaps nibble on a grape or slice of apple. Midge kept herself in trim by turning a few sommersaults; Napper never failed to greet me in the morning no matter what the temperature. So one day when he failed to appear I opened his box at once, knowing that I would find his small body cold and stiff in final sleep. He and

Mr. Perkins died after they had been with us six years. Nix and Becky lived for nine. Jolly Midge held out longer, in her tenth year had what seemed to be a stroke, and from then on danced for visitors in circles, like a waltzing mouse. When she was eleven I noticed she bumped into things, and tests confirmed that she was blind. But her hearing was still good, and she was as merry as ever. Then in her twelfth year she did something very strange. I had given her a pot of earth, thinking it might amuse her, and she did indeed enjoy digging in it, making what appeared to be a rudimentary tunnel. But suddenly she abandoned this project and instead began tamping bits of tissue into the pot of earth, working with almost desperate earnestness, hardly stopping to eat or sleep. Finally it was apparent she was making another nest.

A week passed before this bed was exactly to her liking, with a smooth hollow in the center just big enough for her to lie in, a piece of tissue to one side that could be drawn over her as a cover. When it was at last finished she curled up in it, pulled the cover over her and was quiet. The next day she was still there. Late in the afternoon I carefully lifted the cover to touch her, and she was dead.

She was the last chipmunk to live in our house. Now, when a cat brings one to me, I keep it a few hours to make certain there is no sickness or injury, then about sundown, after the cats have been called indoors, I take it to the woods, far back where I know cats will not venture. Near a boulder with earth under it not too hard for digging, I place a small mound of nuts, to help furnish the new castle. Here life will be shorter, perhaps no more than a day, or an hour; but knowing chipmunks, I know that however long or short, each moment will be enjoyed with zest. And who among us can say that the long life with no spice of peril, only failing senses, is the better one?

Down the road, about a quarter of a mile away, stands a great house, shutters flapping, windows broken, beams sagging, roof open to the wash of sun and rain. There, once, our neighbor Bert lived.

The house did not seem too big in those days. Bert was big, a bull of a fellow who needed plenty of room to roar in; anything smaller would have been a cage. In the village old-timers still tell about how, when he was in his cups, you could hear his bellow all the way down there, over a mile away. That may seem to stretch the truth a bit, but I have corroborative memories; whenever Eric talked to Bert over the telephone, I would go outside to hear both sides of the conversation, Eric's coming through the open door, Bert's booming through his walls and up the road.

Then, too, Bert needed a lot of room to store his possessions. Whenever he went to the village to buy himself a pint, he gave the trip a semblance of propriety, at least in his own eyes, by purchasing also a shirt or a pair of pants. Since the trips were frequent, and he always wore the same old chambray shirt and blue serge suit, the justificatory items really piled up; so did socks, underwear, sheets, patchwork quilts bought at the Ladies' Aid bazaar, where he was a good though somewhat raucous customer, and dishes, cutlery, pots and pans, as well as every kind of tool, nail, screw bolt, wire, nut, or hook to be found in the farmer's catalogue.

This made him a fine neighbor, once you knew how to handle him. In all the years of our association, we never had to buy an electric light bulb. When one burned out we would, just in passing, stop in to say hello to Bert, and while chatting mention ever so casually that we were off to the village to buy a light bulb. "What size?" he'd ask, and going to the dining room, which had been converted to a storeroom, like every other in the house—except the kitchen where he cooked and ate, and the living room where he slept or sat in the rocking chair to read his paper—he would double his great body over one bushel basket after another, to hunt through heaps of clinking bulbs until he found the size we wanted.

In the same way we procured whatever tools we needed, as well as hinges, doorknobs, knives, nails, shovels, even ladders, but only if we just hinted instead of asking straight out; a hard and fast rule to be obeyed meticulously if you wanted to remain in Bert's good graces. Ask for the loan of a bushel basket you could see sitting empty right out in his yard, and staring grimly at that very basket he would tell you he didn't have one, not a single one. Once, before we knew him well, we made the mistake of asking whether we might buy one of his crosscut saws. He didn't speak to us for a week, and of course we didn't get the saw.

Other times, his largess was so unrestrained that we were overwhelmed. In the course of a rambling conversation, Eric happened to express a mild desire for an egg cup, which was passed over then, probably because Bert couldn't make up his mind on the spur of the moment just which storeroom to look into, but the following afternoon Eric returned sheepishly from another visit loaded down with no less than a dozen egg cups, accompanied, logically enough, by a dozen spoons.

Bert was an opinionated, stubborn, hard, ruthless man; we all knew that. He couldn't run the entire world, but he did run the village. Owning not only large tracts of land but also mort- 37 gages on almost all the houses you could point to, he was properly respected; his beliefs were practically out of the bible; his word was close to law. One day as I neared his house I saw him sitting in his rocking chair on the piazza, as he called his front porch, and heard him talking to himself, the way he often did after a trip to the village. Suddenly he roared, "I ain't agonna do it!" This was followed by mumbling that might have been his other self speaking; then he roared again, "I tell you, I ain't agonna do it!" So engrossed was he in this colloquy that he didn't notice me and I slipped past; liquor always sharpened his tongue and made him contemptuous of women, most especially women who liked cats.

Several days later we learned, by a devious route, what the debate was about. Bert held a mortgage on the house of a family in the village; a shiftless lot, to be sure, but also one that had been subjected to an undue amount of hard luck. They had paid nothing at all on the mortgage and were far behind in interest payments. He had every right to forclose, but he did not, to the bewilderment of even the mortgagors, who of course knew nothing about the lonely battle waged between the two selves that alcoholic afternoon.

He hated cats and told me so frequently, because he knew I was partial to them. "Shoot every damn last one I see," he'd shout, then gloat over the mounting color in my cheeks. The more furious I got the more he enjoyed himself, gleefully describing in detail various other methods of exterminating the varmints, as he preferred calling them when he noticed how much more that riled me. Then one evening as we walked toward his house we heard a strange sound on his porch, something like a rusty hinge squeaking, and when we came close were amazed to discover it was Bert crooning in a foolish falsetto, "Here, kitty, kitty, kitty!"

There was no way he could brazen his way out of the situation, not with the bowl of bread and milk in his hands as evidence. Speaking to the dish and not to us, he rumbled a reluctant confession that one of the strays taking shelter in his barn had looked poorly, and he thought it might do with extra rations. Then he went indoors and firmly closed the door, indicating we were not welcome for a chat. I suppose he didn't want to face up to the mockery in my eyes; actually, none was there.

He also hated woodchucks. They got into his garden and ate the tops off the young plants. At one end of the garden was row upon row of rhubarb, which came up all by itself and needed no care. If you wanted truly firm friendship with Bert, it was essential that you should like rhubarb, because he didn't care for it particularly and never knew what to do with it; he would present you with a huge armload, and you had to eat it or else be a darned good liar. The next day you were given an examination; he'd question you at length on how you cooked it, how much sugar you used, whether you had added strawberries like he said, and did you want some more. Unfortunately the woodchucks didn't like rhubarb either, but ate everything else with gusto.

Bert said he'd sit out back some evening with his shotgun, and when they came to feed he'd pepper the lot, maybe with only one shot, at the most, two. No doubt most people, particularly those who owed him money, believed in both his ire and his prowess. We knew better, having taken him unawares one afternoon in a most compromising position, bending over, his immense rump upended like a diving duck's, grubbing in one of the woodchuck burrows.

He was far from pleased to see us. "Oh," he grunted, straightening up, his face beet red either from the stooping or embarrassment. "It's you!" The tone of voice made me think he would have liked very much to pepper us. "Making it bigger," he explained with a shrug, waving a grimy hand toward the burrow. "Darned chuck's got so fat, noticed he had a hard time getting in and out."

That was our neighbor Bert, wondrously complex or foolishly simple, depending on how you looked at him.

He loved the mountains fervently and possessively, as if he had made them himself, and liked nothing better than taking you for a drive through them, should you be properly appreciative. Although more humble, my enthusiasm was as great as his; so, in a way, he was responsible for a further enlargement of our family. On a Sunday afternoon, by a stroke of fate while Eric 39 was in the city (had he been along he'd have urged me to "be sensible," and I might never have known Abbie), a meandering trip took us past a farm where goats were pastured.

Up to then I hadn't seen goats except in pictures. Immediately, irrevocably, I fell in love, which rather pleased Bert. As part of the landscape, were not the goats, too, his handiwork? When I expressed a desire to own one he did not try to dissuade me; to the contrary, he firmed the temptation by offering to teach me how to milk. Possibly he also suggested that one would be lonely, or maybe I thought of this contingency myself. Anyway, I bought two.

Griselda, snow-white, dainty, was as gentle and patient through all the milking lessons as her name implies; Stinky, dirty white, powerful, almost as big as a horse, smelled bad enough to justify his, and was a predisposed killer. All during the year he was with us—we could not say we owned him—I lived in fear. He seldom bucked, but never passed up a chance to rear and try to come down on top of me, the object being to trample with sharp hooves. We could not account for his animosity, for we treated him well; but now, after long association with goats, I think I know what caused it.

The first few months of life seem to be formative for goats. Given kindness then, they go through the rest of their lives without attacking in malice, even when given sufficient provocation. But any abuse during this early period plants in them a hatred, enduring and irreversible, directed toward not only the abuser, but all of mankind. This, you might say, is a rule, and goats live by rules.

There's an old joke about a German immigrant who was caught stealing horses in the early days when our West was still wild. The sheriff says, "You know what the penalty is for stealing horses? We hang you from the nearest tree." To which the German replies, resignedly, "Vateffer is de rule."

Goats are like that, harboring the same unquestioning submission to higher authority. Even pain and death are rules, to which they yield without protest.

Cindy, one of the many that followed those first two, was especially conformant. When she was old, with most of her life behind her and not much ahead, we let her roam during the day, but at five o'clock, for some reason I cannot remember, she was tied to the gatepost. One day shortly after five, we were alarmed by her sudden screaming, and ran out to find her standing near the post. We had forgotten to tie her, and she found this departure from custom unendurable.

In those days it was also the rule that each goat was shut in a separate stall for the night. Just before dark I would go into their yard, call "Places, please," a signal harking back to my days in the theater, and with military precision they would file into the barn, each falling out of line to turn into assigned quarters. There was no dallying, nor any confusion over who belonged where. All I had to do was go along the aisle and flip down the hooks on their gates. However, they had a little rule of their own and did not stay long in the stalls. When I checked later, I always found the gates unlocked and open.

Goats are exceedingly clever, especially when it comes to escaping. I'd venture to say that almost no kind of fence would keep them long in any enclosure; they'd find a weak spot, jump over, crawl under, or squeeze through. What does restrain them is the rule: they know they are supposed to stay inside the fence, therefore they do. So it did not surprise me that they got out of their stalls. What I couldn't understand was how they unlocked the gates.

One evening after I had left them I sneaked back again and peered through the barn window. Soon I saw Penny, the shrewdest of the lot, reach over her gate and with amazing dexterity flip up the hook. She pushed her gate open, then went down the aisle to unlock all the other gates. Goats are gregarious creatures; they like to be together. I thought I'd outwit her and put hasps on the gates, but this turned out to be so much wasted effort. It didn't take her long to discover she could pull out the securing bolts with her teeth and release everyone as before.

Sometimes it happened that their fence, at best no more than a psychological barrier, fell down completely on one side or another, and the temptation of what was beyond eventually became more than they could resist. But, having stepped guiltily into diversion, they did not run away or wander off; all they did was come to the house and stand at the back door, demanding admittance. The ultimate in bliss for any goat, it seems, is to 41 live in a house, like and with human beings. Only one of ours achieved this exalted status, for a short while, and that was Ababa, or Abbie, or Ab.

When I was mad at her she was Ab, ordinarily she was addressed as Abbie, but if I felt particular affection for her she became Ababa; and don't think she didn't know the difference. The first would produce on her face a look of guilt or stubbornness, depending upon her own mood, while the last made her raise a reciprocal hoof, with grace and dignity, and come as close to purring as a goat could.

She was one of Cindy's offspring. Cindy was a good, conscientious, devoted mother to whatever bucks she drew out of the celestial grab bag. The does she either ignored or tossed aside as being of no importance or, perhaps, as possible future rivals. Who can fathom a goat's reasoning? Obscure as to origin, the discrimination was nevertheless inflexible, so when Buster was born he was loved with a loving tongue, crooned over and cuddled, while Ababa, following soon after, was nudged into a corner by a contemptuous nose.

I was the one who dried her off and crooned to her; I cuddled her in my arms and took her into the house, made a warm bed for her and robbed her brother of some milk to feed her. I was the one who set her on wobbly legs and murmured encouragement as she took her first steps, who guided and protected her and played games that would give her strength and stamina. That was how I became her mother. To her there was no difference between us, other than that I was older and bigger and wiser. I was another goat—or she another human. Again, I cannot be sure just which way the reasoning went.

Introduced to her brother and the rest of the goats, she lifted a disdainful nose and would have nothing to do with them. But step for step she followed me like a faithful dog, and whenever I sat down she was on my lap, grunting and puffing with pleasure, gazing up at me with eloquent eyes that drifted out of focus and closed and struggled to open again, and closed finally in contented surrender to sleep.

When she was stronger we took walks together, once each day going down to Bert's house to call for the mail he'd brought from the post office. She trotted primly at my side, intrigued by the many sights and smells along the way but never straying, not at all perturbed by the cars that swept past, confident of my ability to protect her.

In Bert's house I would sit in the rocker to chat for a while, and she would hop onto my lap to listen to the conversation, looking from one to the other of us as we spoke, as if she were following and understanding every word. Only if we talked too long she would lose interest. Her head would bobble and nod, and with a sigh she would rest it on my arm, to sleep until I roused her for the trip home.

Four times a day she came into our house to have her bottle, on my lap. She loved the ritual of this perhaps more than the milk itself, and insisted it must be followed even after she was munching grass and leaves with capable teeth. She grew too big for my lap. No matter how we shifted and adjusted she would no longer fit. Then she stood beside the chair to drink her milk, demolishing a nipple each time, and afterward rested her head on my lap for a while, in remembrance of her babyhood, and in protest against growing up.

At last, fortunately, another love came into her life. She grew enamored of Percy, the herd buck, and although she would not desert me for him, whenever I went into the house and closed the door behind me, she no longer shrieked complaints and tried to kick the door down, but instead went mooning after Percy. A big, magnificent fellow, he was, unlike his father, most amiable. Willingly, although somewhat sheepishly, he dispensed with dignity to humor Abbie and join in a silly game.

Almost all the other goats, in youthful exuberance, had teased me somehow. Few of them could resist hopping up whenever I stooped over to caper on my back. Catching me in the same position, Percy dearly loved to take a bite at the provocatively soft part of my anatomy thus made prominent. Sam snatched things out of my pockets, once a letter just written and about to be mailed. I had to chase him all over the yard to retrieve it, much crumpled, and wondered what the recipient must have thought of such a sorry looking missive. Abbie played none of these tricks on me; she was a proper, dignified, almost solemn companion, deferring high-spirited mischievousness until she could provoke Percy into mock battle or a game of tag.

Yet she was not perfect; two faults she had were particularly distressing. Although Percy bellowed in protest and I shouted warnings, she could not be kept from wandering out on the road, where trips with me had accustomed her to traveling safely, and there she challenged all cars to run her down. The other fault, even though most flattering, gave me considerable discomfort. She was terribly jealous. I had to take care not to pay too much attention to any of the other goats—Percy was the one exception —or the cats, the dog, even Eric, if I were not to become the recipient of her wrath; unlike most animals, she put the blame and punishment not on the object of my interest but on me, exactly where it belonged.

One time she definitely became Ab was when a friend paid a visit. It was a lovely summer day and we sat outside, on a flat rock in the field, to talk. Abbie stood near us listening to the conversation, as she had done when she was little. But, as then, she grew bored after a while and, remembering too well, tried to fit herself on my lap. The sun was warm, there was entirely too much of her, and I pushed her away. She prowled around us, every so often coming in to nudge me, reminding me she was still there. I kept shoving her off, and finally said impatiently, "Oh, Abbie, go away!" That did it. Looking terribly hurt, she trotted off, and for a minute, but only a minute, I felt remorseful. Then something like a sledge-hammer hit me in the back and tossed me off the rock. Since none of her blandishments had diverted my attention, she had to show me there were more persuasive means at her command.

In time she bore kids, and she was a good mother, efficient, conscientious, but subscribing to no slobbery nonsense about a miracle having occurred. The kids were there, obviously hers, and she was not one to shirk duties, especially if I praised her for fulfilling them. But her love was still given to Percy and to me, and she did not fuss when the offspring were taken from her.

Then wild animals brought in a disease that killed Percy and left Abbie sterile, and she had no more kids of her own, but no lessening of responsibility either. All the kids belonging to the younger does seemed to prefer her company, except when they were hungry, and she became as good a foster mother as she had been a mother. The kids clambered over her, chewed on her ears and beard, slept nestled against her, trotted beside her while she grazed. She kept order, talked to them, stopped fights, and taught them how to dance.

This was a performance we never tired of watching. We could almost hear her giving instructions: "Come, up on your hind legs! Nice and tall, forelegs close to the body, chin tucked in, head turned a bit to one side. That's it! Sway a little, this way, that way, and waggle your feet. Good. Now down, and *charge*! No, not too hard. This is only a game. Then quickly, quickly, swing around, kicking your heels; to the left, to the right, faster, higher! A twist and a flourish at the end, and once more, *up*!

Actually, the game was more than that. Abbie was teaching the youngsters the art of self defense. Each posture, each movement had purpose: rearing, to trample; flailing the hooves, to protect the belly; lowering the chin, to guard the throat; turning the head, for better vision. Swaying gave snakelike mobility for striking; charging, the momentum and power to down an adversary. The swift circling with kicking heels would take care of dogs and other predators that almost always attack from the rear, to hamstring their prey. Having learned this dance, a goat of almost any size is a formidable adversary; a really big one can be deadly. Knowing this, an experienced farmer will put a goat in with his herd of sheep to protect them. But the dance itself, so gay and droll and full of grace, was entrancing.

For the kids, for all the goats, Abbie had become a wise, benign matriarch. In a way she was that to me also; she had begun to talk to me, too, in affectionate little grunts much like those she addressed to the kids, as if our roles were now reversed, she the elder, I the younger. When the brown earth turned green in spring I said, "Come, Abbie," and she led her charges to the pasture. In fall when the first snow hung in the air I said, "Come, Abbie," and she took them back to winter quarters in the barn. She showed the young ones the big, flat, sun-warmed rock, the cool hollow under the trees, where to drink and where to find shelter when rain fell. She told them when it was time to stand at the fence to wait for the evening feeding. Unlike their jittery mothers she was placid, indulgent, alert to protect them but never an alarmist. This must have been what attracted them to her, but I like to think they were aware of something more, a sturdy, 45 endearing quality, not readily definable, that made me love her also. She was, dependably, comfortably, unalterably—Abbie.

Years passed; generation after generation of kids came and went. The house where Abbie had come to get her milk was enlarged, a back porch was added; inside, furniture was replaced, as was the old wood stove by a space heater; the cats were different from those she had met and greeted with a friendly touch of the nose; Muff, whom she had known as a young dog, had left us. So had Eric. In the midst of all this change, there was Abbie, unchanged.

One way or another, the herd of goats diminished, until only Molly's Samson was born in the spring. Pure white, handsome, reminding me of his early forebear, Stinky, Samson looked upon Abbie with pale blue newborn eyes and at once, it seemed, gave her his heart—a pretty big heart. As soon as he could walk properly he was toddling after her. His mother became only a milk-bar; I didn't even exist. As always, Abbie was patient, allowing him to paw and nuzzle and chew and climb up on her back, but she did not teach him to dance. When I looked in the book where all the births were recorded, I knew why.

There was hers, put down in browning ink fourteen years before. It did not seem so long since I had held her on my lap, sitting in the rocking chair chatting with Bert. But it was true, Bert was dead, the rocking chair gone, and Abbie was old.

I resolved to devote the summer to her. Unless it rained, which was seldom, we went walking together, just as in the good days when she was young. I would take my book or sewing, or pencil and paper if I happened to be working on something, and call "Abbie?" At once she was with me; so was Samson. It was a terrible summer of drouth that turned the grass to dust; of worms that infested and devoured the leaves of bushes and trees. We had to roam far to find suitable grazing. When we came to a good patch of goldenrod or Quaker lady or red raspberries, Abbie's favorites, I would sit on a rock to read or mend, or think and write; she would browse, with head turned now and then to make sure I was still there. On another rock nearby Samson folded up to gaze at Abbie and wait, ready on the instant to move if she did.

In fall, in spite of the drouth, there was a good crop of apples and we did not walk so far, spending the greater part of the day in an old orchard just above the house. Once in a while Abbie had to sneak off to show Samson the road, but most of the time, until the apples were gone and the wind blew cold and the ground froze, the three of us were together.

Then came winter, the worst in memory, with high winds and blustery snow and bitter cold, reaching an unbearable climax in a three-day storm that sent the temperature to thirty-five below zero and whipped winds up to eighty miles an hour. It is possible to live, even get about, in such a wind; a temperature of thirty-five below can also be endured, if the air is still. But a combination of the two is something that simply cannot be; yet it was. Huddled with the cats near the stove, I worried about Abbie, and at three in the morning, at the height of the storm, had to go out to her. My intention was to bring her back to the house, never mind what was proper, but as I faced the wind's violence I knew she'd never make it. I almost didn't myself. Then inside the barn I found her better off than I had dared hope, stamping her feet to warm them, but actually shivering less than the others.

The following day the wind died down, the temperature rose, the sun shone. Abbie stood basking in its warmth, head lowered in somnolence; when I offered apples and bread she came running to get her share, always the first piece, and more than the others. She looked well as ever; yet shortly after I had returned to the house I heard her calling, with a peculiar urgency that meant something was wrong, and hurried out to find her slumped in a corner of the barn, one side of her body icy cold.

Half carrying, half dragging, I got her out of the barn, away from the others, into the shed where the hay was stored. I covered her with a blanket, gave her food and wine. She ate readily, but her head bobbled over the dish, just as it had fourteen years before, when she was a baby sucking on her bottle. Every hour after that I went to look at her. She slept. She raised her head when I approached. She sat up, flicked her ears and held them erect, and at last she greeted me at the door. She could walk again. She was better, and to prove it, raised a hoof with delicate grace to meet my hand.

Fate sometimes plays cruel jokes. The next day was dark and cold, the wind was back, and Abbie was worse. She still could walk, but feebly, and she would not eat. With the tips of my 47 fingers lightly touching the back of her neck—all that was ever needed—I guided her out of the shed, to the house. On the back porch I made a bed for her, and I left the door open, so that she could see into the house and share its warmth.

She lay content, while I waited for the veterinarian who never came, until late in the afternoon. Then suddenly she was on her feet, swaying. She had made up her mind to something; there was that old stubborn expression I knew so well. She took a few tottering steps to test her legs, and walked into the house.

Goats have astounding memories. Once I gave away a doe, and five years later when her new owner died, took her back again. She leaped out of the truck that delivered her and went running to the barn with a yelp of joy. After five years of exile, she was *home* again.

So I had no doubt that Abbie remembered the house, although she had not entered it for fourteen years. She went first to the chair—another, but like the old one and in the same place— where she had sat on my lap to be fed. She went to my bunk, on which she had pranced long ago with the cats. She went to the stove—a space burner now, but in the same position—beside which she had dozed, her legs folded and tucked under her body like a cat's.

At the very end of his life, Percy had somehow found the strength to make the long trip from the barn, where for days he had lain dying, down the hill to the pasture, where his does were. He stared and stared at them, one after the other; then he fell, and died. Now I knew Abbie was saying goodbye to the house in the same way. She looked at everything for a long time; then returned to stand beside her chair. Her head drooped. She was very tired.

My fingertips on her neck, I guided her back to her bed on the porch. She sank down, closed her eyes and slept, heavily, one hour, and another. Finally I went out and knelt beside her, took the old head in my arms and spoke her name, the loving one, Ababa. She had to respond. She opened her eyes, fought to keep them open, her gaze out of focus, and tried to grunt an answer. Instead there came from her throat a long, terrible, human-animal wail that surely would have embarrassed her if she had heard it; above all, she was a lady. But she could not have heard. Life went out of her with that cry.

I buried her in the snow, in the night, when we could be alone together, and perhaps that was selfish of me. In the hostile cold and wind of the grieving day, Samson hung around the back door hour after hour, calling to her. He had seen her go into the house, he could not understand why she would not come out again. There was a hole in his life also, but not so big as the one in mine.

We never knew what to do with the kids. The does we could keep, or sell, after having made certain the buyers wanted milk, not meat. But the bucks definitely had to go, and where? Italians are very fond of goat meat, which is called chevon, and particularly at Easter time will pay good prices, even fight over well-nourished kids. Once, when we had a record crop of bucks, we did harden our hearts and sell three for such a purpose. I had bad dreams for weeks, and still cannot recall that time of defection without distress.

The trouble was, I told Eric, we gave them names and so made them individuals. We should look upon them as no more than meat from the time they were born, refrain from associating with them, leave them nameless. Unfortunately they all developed personalities anyway, and capered into our unwilling hearts. Well, I myself would kill them, I said; at least that way they would go gently and not suffer through inept slaughtering. But I could not. We tried giving them away, begging people in the village to take one or another. "He would make a fine companion for your youngster," we would say, or, "You could teach him to pull a cart; he'd be useful." But in the end these also ended up like the rest, on the dinner table.

Pepper, an engaging black-and-white fellow, was a particular problem because I had used him as the subject of a picture book, and our long hours of companionship while I photographed had produced mutual affection. Yet he could not remain with us. In a few months his presence would be resented by Percy, just then in his prime and jealously possessive of both his humans and his small herd of does. We pondered, and finally Eric offered a solution: August Lindemann, perhaps?

Down the mountain, seventeen miles away, a man named Roland Lindemann owned a small game farm, about a hundred acres of land and fifteen white-tailed deer. Today this is an immense, awesome enterprise, the Catskill Game Farm, famed the world over for its fine collection of rare animals. But in those earlier days it was, I think, more fun; there were few visitors, in contrast to the ten thousand per day it now receives, and one could really get acquainted with the deer. We would drive down to spend an afternoon with them, well supplied with bread, crackers, carrots, and apples, which they liked to nose out of our pockets; then around four o'clock we left them to go up a steep hill, along a meandering dirt road, to another place called the Catskill Zoo. There August Lindemann, Roland's father, would hurry out of his house to greet us, beard waving, eyes twinkling, handclasp firm and friendly; and the soft voice, used to conversing with animals, would caress the words, "Ya, ya, welcome!"

It wasn't much of a zoo; rabbits, guinea pigs, chipmunks, squirrels, skunks, raccoons, birds, one great horned owl. Past the owl he took us quickly, with a deprecatory wave of the hand. "You would not like. I do not like. Live mice, he must have. I let him go, I think." But all the others were cared for lovingly. Cages for birds had been built around large trees, "to make them feel at home," wire mesh enclosing the chipmunks went deep into the ground so they might tunnel under rocks, construct castles, just as if they were still free. Rabbits were quartered in roomy, spotless hutches with long runways; each raccoon and skunk had a private dwelling. But there was more for us to see. He had to take us to his garden, row upon row of tall-growing color; up and 51 down the rows he would go, touching as he commented, "This I give the name of my old friend Ludwig . . . poor fellow, he's dead now. This I call Helga. She is like a woman, no? All dressed up. And this one, so important looking—"with a shrug and a laugh— "I name after our President. Why not, eh?"

We loved the Catskill Zoo and its jolly, modest owner. Even now, so many years later, I can see him quite clearly, stooping at the edge of the road to select choice grasses for his rabbits, serene as the sunlit summer day; and if I were asked to define true happiness, I might describe him and the life he led. I was glad that when death took him, it did so quietly and gently, as he had lived.

We drove down the mountain that fall, past the game farm, directly to the little zoo, and the whole of the way Pepper lay without moving on my lap, uttering no protest, not even questioning, his eyes showing only acceptance. "What must be, must be," they said. Goats are fatalists.

August Lindemann was delighted to see him. "Ach, what a nice fellow! Beautiful! Ya, I take good care. Now, you must have something in exchange. Whatever you see, you like, you take."

We looked at all the guinea pigs, rabbits, birds, skunks, raccoons, like children offered an assortment of candy unable to make a choice, almost decided on an exotic guinea pig with long silky fur, then came to the lovely Himalayan rabbits, and went no further. Gleaming white and dainty, they had black noses, black ears, black stockings, and black pompoms for tails. "But one is lonely, that is not good," Lindemann said. "You take the pair, eh?"

That was how we came to have the rabbits.

Their hutch still stands and is used occasionally as a temporary shelter for some animal in need of care; this summer it has housed the three orphaned skunks. Loppy, the buck lived for six years, a good life for a rabbit; Lolly was with us longer. Next to their hutch are their graves, grown over with forget-me-nots. Of their many offspring some were sold, some were kept and died in due time, until only two were left, sisters so alike that I could not tell them apart and called them, simply, the Lolly Babies.

When these two were ten years old—an extraordinary age for

rabbits—we came to the severe winter in which Abbie died. They hadn't a chance of survival out of doors in such protracted bitter cold; I took them from their hutch and brought them into the house, where for a while they lived isolated in the bedroom; like most people, I believed cats and rabbits would not coexist amicably, unless the latter were inside the former. Between chores, I set to remodeling the old chipmunk cage, and when it was finished, put the rabbits in it on the porch, which was glassed in and fairly warm. During the day they had to stay in the cage. At night, when the cats were indoors, they were given the freedom of the porch. Sometimes I went out and sat with them for a while, and so, as we became acquainted, I discovered they were not at all alike.

Lolly One, gay, inquisitive, venturesome, always came to nudge under my hand, asking to be petted, and when I sat down, hopped on my lap to snuggle. Lolly Two was shy, but followed with trust wherever her sister led. Between them was evidence of great affection. They slept together, ate together, starting and stopping simultaneously; they played together, hopping around in mild games of tag, and were visibly distressed by even a momentary separation.

Throughout the winter they enjoyed the comfort of the porch. Then, just as the world was changing its coat to green, and life had become easier for all of us, Lolly One sickened. She grew thin, sat hunched in a corner, could not be tempted to eat even the first tender sprouts of clover I had searched out. Lolly Two sat with her, pressed close against the listless body, as if to give it strength, and ate very little, only just enough to stay alive. Finally one morning I found Lolly One in the middle of the floor, still breathing but helpless, her faithful sister huddled over her. Evidently she had had a stroke; one side of her body was paralyzed.

I fed her warm cereal with a dropper, while Lolly Two hopped desperately around my feet; then rigged up a sling to support her, with enough give so that she could rest if she wished. Lolly Two sat near the sling in constant attendance; warming, washing, keeping her sister company. Gradually the invalid grew stronger; she ate again, and for the first time the two had a difference of opinion. Lolly One acquired a most unorthodox fond-   53 ness for sliced bananas, which Lolly Two found so repulsive that she tried to sweep them away with an offended nose.

For a while each day the sling was removed; Lolly One could stand, even get around a little. Then came another stroke. She was eleven; it was time for her to go. On a spring morning that was dark even though new green glittered under a bright sun, I took her on my lap and gave her the pill that would set her free. At my feet Lolly Two sat waiting for the return of her companion. When instead I put the small body into a box and carried the box away, she went quite mad. For hours she hopped wildly, around and around, only stopping now and then to poke and search in the most unlikely crevices, persistently, as if hope could bring back the dead. Only toward sundown did she become quiet, too quiet. All that night and the next day and the next, she sat with her head turned into a corner, her back toward the world, and all food was refused. Could a rabbit die of grief? It seemed that she would.

What made me think of the brick I don't know. Only the day before I had come upon one, and being a zealous salvager, had wondered how it might be put to use. I brought it in, washed it, wrapped it in an old shawl of mine, even gave it a name. "Here's Oscar," I told Lolly, putting the brick down beside her. She sniffed, gave it a nudge, snuggled against it and began licking it ardently. I pushed her food closer, and she ate and ate, making up for all the days she had missed. During the weeks that followed her devotion to Oscar remained constant, and she washed him so much that she wore a hole through the shawl. She was once more content, but watching her fuss over this cold, lifeless object, I was distressed. Even though her life might be brought to an abrupt end, I had to offer her better company than a brick. So one morning I did not close her cage when I let the cats on the porch. As the first of them hesitated, then went into the cage, I winced. But what I had feared did not happen. The cat touched noses with the rabbit, gave her a friendly lick, and turned away. One by one all the others stopped in to pay their respects and having done so, went out to check on how the world had got through the night.

Cricket soon came back. She was close to her time and cutting down on activity. As if it had been her custom, she went straight into the rabbit cage, lay down beside Lolly and kept her company in a midmorning nap. A few days later her kittens were born, in the rabbit cage, and there they were raised, with Lolly acting as baby-sitter whenever Cricket went for a stroll. Laved by two dissimilar tongues, the kittens' fur shone with cleanliness. They particularly enjoyed playing with Lolly's long ears, and evidently grew up believing themselves to be at least part rabbit; the first solid food they ate was clover. At the same time Lolly must have become convinced that she was something other than a rabbit; she acquired a fondness for dog chow.

Of course the time came when the kittens, lured by Cricket's calling, ventured out through the swinging door, and I had to start worrying about Lolly being lonely again. On rainy days so many cats squeezed into the cage to sleep away the dull hours that the rabbit was practically invisible, only one ear or the tip of her nose showing somewhere in the heap. But as soon as the weather was more favorable they deserted her; all, that is, except a little gray one named Mia. Mia was on the dwarfish side, therefore timid, and a homebody. After a while it became evident that she had adopted the rabbit as her very own. In the morning she would hurry outside to dig a hole and squat, her eyes on the house, and as soon as she had properly heaped earth over the hole, she would come back in to Lolly. She washed the rabbit, taking care to get well inside the odd long ears. She scrubbed herself, her tongue going back to Lolly's fur every once in a while for an extra lick, and having finished her chores, lay down, curled around her companion, her chin resting on the rabbit's head. For a while their eyes would stay open; they were not sleeping, just enjoying the comfort of being together. If I spoke, Mia's purring became at once more audible, and so did Lolly's soft, contented grunting. But, asleep or awake, Mia remained alert. Any untoward noise, a cat squabble outside, a dog barking, footsteps approaching, brought her immediately to her feet, on guard, and Lolly's head was thrust under her belly for protection. They had only one slight difference of opinion. Whenever I heard Mia cry out in protest during the night, I knew Lolly was trying again to pull out her fur, to make a nest.

In the winter of her twelfth year Lolly began to fail. She grew thin and lethargic. Her coat became scraggly, her appetite capricious. Standing over her I pleaded silently, "Only live until spring. Just until spring, Lolly." One last time I wanted her to enjoy the first sprouts of clover; and I hoped the warmth and quickening out of doors might make Mia forget more readily.

As if through my will Lolly lived, from day to day, week to week, until the winter winds stopped blowing, the air turned balmy, the snow melted, a shimmer of green spread over the fields. I went searching, found a few shoots of clover and brought them home in triumph; Lolly ate, hopped up and down to touch my hand, begging for more. Each day I rambled through the fields, and counted the clover leaves I was able to find: ten, then twenty, then thirty. Lolly expected them, came to meet me to get them.

Then one morning I found the faithful Mia curled around a cold, stiff body. Lolly had met my terms. Old as she was, she had spun out her life until spring; beyond that she could not go.

I wish I might say Mia found solace; in truth, I cannot. For quite a while I left the cage on the porch and put in fresh hay daily, as if Lolly were still there; and as if she were still there, Mia remained in the cage, not sleeping, not purring, only staring with wide eyes at her loneliness. At last I took the cage away and gave her a box, with a blanket in it. There she lies now, a remote circle closed against the world; but within, who knows what memories keep her company?

When the house was packed with the dog and all the cats, the hutches with rabbits, the barn with goats, Eric looked from our bank balance to a sheaf of bills and said, "No more animals, now. There's a limit." Even when Bert told us about the raccoons Eric said, "No more animals. However," he added, "I don't suppose it would do any harm to go look at them." And Bert grinned knowingly.

A family of five babies had been found by woodsmen and turned over to the game warden who lived at the end of our road. The game warden said the mother must have been killed, possibly when her den tree was felled, more likely by an encounter with a porcupine; all the young were carrying quills.

He took them out of the box, five droll brown woolly balls that scuttled in every direction, chuckling softly. One came toward me, reached up tiny hands to touch my leg. "I'll take this one," I said. Eric already had chosen his; murmuring endearments and chuckling with pleasure, he held it cradled in his arms, bank balance and bills forgotten.

We knew little enough about raccoons, only what we had read in books. They were nocturnal, arboreal, expert fishermen;

their front feet resembled, indeed, were used much like hands; they always washed their food before eating it. They had a sometimes fatal weakness for bright objects; knowing this, a trapper would use bright pieces of metal for bait. Their food, according to the books, consisted of nuts, fruit, green corn, shell fish, frogs, turtles, birds and their eggs; no mention was made of what to feed baby raccoons with only buds of teeth showing. We had to experiment. Given a bowl of milk, the two daintily dipped in their hands, tried to scoop the milk into their mouths; when this didn't work they turned the whole business into a game, paddling and splashing happily until the bowl was empty, the milk running all over the floor, and they still had nothing in their stomachs except what was obtained from the industrious fur washing that followed. We thought of Pablum, mixed some with milk to make a fairly solid paste, and this they ate with zest, dipping out small portions, rolling them into balls between the palms of their hands, and popping the balls into their mouths.

Our agreement with the game warden was that as soon as the raccoons were old enough to take care of themselves we would release them; in the state of New York it is against the law to keep raccoons captive. We decided to advance this unhappy date—to look at a baby raccoon is to fall instantly in love—and give them their freedom immediately. After they had eaten and we had extracted their quills, an operation they submitted to with protesting squeals but no ill will, we took them outside, and thereupon discovered we had become parents.

Wherever we went the raccoons patted behind us, much as they would if they had been with their mother in the woods, not silently but with constant chattering: to the garden, where they fingered the petals of flowers and made clumsy, fortunately ineffectual passes at a bee, up one path, down another, and finally to the brook. There the venturesome male we called Hansel plunged in to swim from shore to shore and back again, while the more timid Gretel stood watching with no more than her toes immersed, until excitement over her brother's triumphant crossing made her leap up and down like a cheer leader, splashing water all over herself and her doting foster parents. Then, following us, they returned home, toiled up the stair mountain, and in the house made two sets of wet handprints across the floor to their box. There they washed themselves dry, napped, awoke to play a wild, noisy game, tumbling over each other wrestling, nipping, shrieking, snorting, growling, and suddenly they were asleep again.

For a few weeks this was their life; then they became less dependent upon us. The lower part of our screen door had been cut out and a swinging door put in, to facilitate the many exits and entrances of the cats; Muff had used it also, and so, to some extent, had Abbie—only her head would go through the opening. Once discovered, the door fascinated the raccoons; gleefully they plunged out and in, over and over, out to take a look at the world, in again to make sure we were still in the house as we should be.

If by chance we were not, they sought us out with loud complaints, and having found us, dogged our footsteps like neophyte sleuths. As long as we were merely going to the brook for water, or the woodlot for logs, they were welcome enough, but their persistent attendance did make shopping difficult. We'd sneak out of the house, tiptoe to the road, not daring to speak, and having gone a fair distance would congratulate ourselves on having got safely away, only to hear a sudden "Chirrrr! Chirrrr!" behind us, and there would be two brown rubber balls bouncing along to catch up with us. We'd have to retrace our steps, one riding on each of our shoulders, put them in their box with some of the peppermints they dearly loved, wait for them to fall asleep, then try again, stealing away like thieves, with apprehensive backward glances. I found myself sympathizing with true mother raccoons, who must have shopping problems also.

Bold Hansel was the first to climb a tree, the towering maple at the side of our house. Timidly, Gretel followed, and for hours they swung through the branches like monkeys, or lay spraddled over one, toying with the leaves. Then they had to explore the brook. Hansel snuffled upstream along the bank, Gretel snuffled unwillingly after him, and both disappeared in the woods. At first they came back from these excursions almost immediately, calling "Hm? Hm? Hm?" which is the raccoon cry for reassurance that always brings mamma running to the rescue, and to which I responded with the same alacrity. But as they came to know the woods their absences gradually lengthened, until a 59 new routine had been established. In the morning, right after breakfast, they would leave the house to spend the day in the woods; at sundown they would return for their supper, then play around the house until it was time for bed.

Again, Hansel was first in coming to the conclusion that such a life was no proper one for a raccoon who is, after all, supposed to be a night animal. After supper one evening he went back out through the swinging door. Gretel followed dubiously, and I followed her. For a while they played just in front of the house, tumbling like kittens. But suddenly, noiselessly, Hansel slipped into the darkness under the trees and vanished. Gretel came to where I was sitting on the steps, put her hands on my knee and softly trilled some message. Although I did not understand, I answered and stroked her head; then she also drifted away, a shadow melting into the shadows Hansel had entered. Now our promise to the game warden has been kept, I thought.

The two raccoons had no more need of us. I knew they were supplementing the food we gave them with grubs and berries found in the woods. Their teeth had grown long and sharp, their hands, still soft-palmed, as they always would be, were equipped with heavy, curved non-retractable claws, efficient weapons for defense against almost all enemies, except men with guns, or a pack of dogs. When I went back into the house I said to Eric, "I suppose we've seen the last of them." But I was wrong.

At midnight the little swinging door slammed, and slammed again. There they were, back home. We were so glad that we gave them an unscheduled snack: milk, peanuts, and for dessert, a marshmallow each. After Hansel had downed his share he prowled around, coming every once in a while to stare into my eyes with such sadness that I wanted to put my arms around him, to console him. But this he did not want; it was some other need that made him restless. He put his hands on the sill of the swinging door, poked his head out, was still for a moment, sorting out reports the wind was bringing from the woods, came at last to a decision, and departed. Gretel started after him, changed her mind and turned toward me. That night for the first time she slept not in their box, but on my bed.

The next day she puttered around the house, not knowing what to do without Hansel's guidance, until I took pity on her, called Muff, and went for a walk through the woods. That pleased her. As Muff and I strolled along the bank of the brook she paddled in it, and when we turned to go through the wood-lot she climbed up and down trees, sometimes pursuing or being pursued by the cats that had caught up with us. I started back, thinking she might like to stay there playing in the trees, but before Muff and I had gone far she was with us, then ahead of us, racing the cats to see who could get to the house first.

The rest of the day she napped, or played quietly with the toys I had given her, an assortment of buttons, spools, bits of metal and, most prized of all, a long hollow bone handed down from Muff. Her favorite game was to put a button in one end of the bone and retrieve it from the other. If an overlarge button got stuck in the middle she was delighted; here was a problem to work on. Upending the bone, she would shake it, and if neither this strategy nor the efforts of her nimble fingers dislodged the button, she would blow through the bone, to her great glee making a hooting noise that sounded something like a foghorn.

But toward dusk she put away all the toys, in what we came to call her treasure chest, the farthest corner underneath my bunk, and began to pace up and down, going frequently to the swinging door to look out, and turning away again. The night was calling to her but she was afraid to go into it alone.

To distract her, Eric put on heavy work gloves and invited her to play a game of roughhouse; with alacrity she accepted. When she sprang at him, he threw her over on her back, and in mock savagery she tore at his gloved hands. Watching, fascinated, I could understand why this animal is so feared by the hunter and his dogs. Although a confirmed pacifist, a frightened, enraged raccoon might very well tear a dog to shreds, and do considerable damage to the hunter as well.

Just in the middle of this game we were suddenly transfixed, then precipitated into action by a sound outside the open window. "Chirrrrrrrr! Chirrrrrrrr!" The cats ran for cover, Eric, Muff, and I made for the window, Gretel, the cleverest among us, went to the swinging door and stood beside it, sending out a delicate little answering "Chirrrrrr?"

Yes, it was Hansel. He had climbed the hemlock growing close by the house to look through the window, to make sure 61 everything was as he had left it before he entered this former home of his. Reassured, he came down, walked around to the front door and accepted Gretel's invitation to enter. With him came an overwhelming stench. Hansel, the adventurer, had been taught a lesson by the woods: sharp though his teeth and claws might be, they were not match for the weapon carried by the skunk.

He backed away as we approached, keeping a prudent distance from us, evidently only too conscious of his unwelcome odor; and when we laughed, he looked hurt. We put down a bowl of milk. He went to it eagerly, but after a few sips, gulped and went back out through the swinging door. Gretel hesitated, then went out also. Evidently the smell was not displeasing to her; for a while she played with him as on the previous night, and again they both vanished.

I worried. From then on there was always this worry, not so much for Hansel, who had chosen uncertain life in the woods over that we offered, but for the timorous Gretel who was lured almost against her will away from safety, into peril. However, a definitive routine had been agreed upon. During the day Gretel stayed with us, going for a walk in the woods, playing with her toys, having her game of roughhouse with Eric; her nights belonged to Hansel. Each evening, as soon as darkness made the trip safe, he would come to the house, climb the tree to make sure he was welcome, walk in to get his supper, then take Gretel off on their date. Always at midnight he brought her back, delivered her at the door and departed. From then until morning she slept on my bed, starting at the lower corner and gradually working up, until with a nudge of the nose she asked me to lift the covers. When I did she crawled under, put her head on the pillow, slipped her soft little hand into mine, and her purring was a deep rumble against my ear. Evidently both of us slept quietly; often in the morning I awoke to find we had held hands all through the night.

Gradually the nightly excursions with Hansel sloughed away her fear; she grew bold also and added to my worries by making occasional tours all by herself during the day, always ending up in some mischief. She loved people, never mind what they thought of her, and sought them out. She visited Bert, climbed

62

up on his bed and lay spread on her back contentedly playing with her toes until a desperate telephone call brought us to his rescue. She went still farther away, to the milkman who lived beyond Bert; he was building a barn, and the fine lot of noise he made must have attracted her. She watched with interest while he sawed and hammered, disconcerted him by thrusting an inquisitive nose between the descending hammer and the nail, or just under the blade of the saw. Again, we had to go down and fetch her. Then, for variety, she went up and across the road, to get acquainted with the people who ran a small boarding house.

It was late summer, the boarding house still had a few guests, who on this particular day were gathered in the living room, playing cards. Gretel walked through the open door and stood on her hind legs to stare at them, probably overjoyed to see so many people all at once. The people, however, were far from pleased to see her; in fact, being city people, they didn't even know *what* they were seeing. She advanced toward them, with one accord they rose, scattering their cards over the floor, and fled to the dining room. Most of them huddled in a corner, but a few brave ones stayed near the door to poke cautious heads around the jamb, and they were the ones who reported to us later.

Gretel fingered some of the fallen cards, drew herself up tall, and sniffed. On the table was a bowl of candy. She climbed a chair, helped herself to a caramel, returned to the floor, arranged her rump comfortably under her, and was preoccupied for some time, taking the paper off the caramel. Having done so, she ate with much smacking and chewing to get the tenacious substance off her teeth, then considered the problem of what to do with the wrapper. Far from addicted to neatness, she nevertheless liked to hide things. Wandering around, she at last came to the sofa and discovered a small hole, probably made by a careless smoker; she enlarged it suitably, tucked the paper well down into it, and went off satisfied.

Not all raccoons wash their food—she never did hers—but they like to keep their hands clean, and Gretel's were somewhat sticky. Her nose led her unerringly to water, past the people huddled in the dining room, into the kitchen. The sink was inaccessible, barricaded by two women, frozen in the act of washing and drying dishes, staring at her wide-eyed with disbelief. But there was another source of water. She went to the stove, fortunately cool, climbed up its sides, stood next to the teakettle and daintily dipped in her hands. Again, we were telephoned. It had got so that whenever we heard our ring while Gretel was absent, we were at once distraught, knowing we would hear some tale of woe.

But the days were growing shorter. The leaves of the trees, having blazed, fluttered down to carpet the ground with orange and red and yellow. In the morning there was sometimes frost, and at night a hint of snow. Here in the Catskills raccoons hibernate. Crawling into caves or hollow trees as soon as the first real snow falls, they remain curled up there until around the middle of March, or February if the winter has been mild, when it is time for them to mate. No doubt Hansel already had chosen the den where he would hole up. But Gretel? Where would she sleep, with him in the woods, or with us in our house? The choice turned out to be one she did not have to make. On the first day of the hunting season gunshots echoed throughout the woods. That evening Hansel did not come to take Gretel for her walk, and we never saw him again.

We missed him, of course, and were saddened, but he had grown so independent of us that our lives were little changed, except for that period just before dusk when Gretel grew restless. From window to door to window she paced, back and forth, back and forth, and nothing could distract her. She was waiting for Hansel; grieving also, I think. Raccoons form strong attachments, and like goats, have long memories.

Although she showed no signs of hibernating, we provided for that possibility by giving her a box on a high shelf, with an old sweater of mine for bedding. She loved this retreat, respected by the cats as private property and therefore all her own. Each day after we had returned from our walk—short now because of the danger of our becoming a hunter's target—she would climb up to spend the afternoon there, washing and grooming herself, singing softly. Her little song, a kind of humming and crooning and mellow chuckling, like friendly water flowing among rocks, was a soothing, lovely sound.

She was fussy about her bed. Every so often she had to take the sweater out and shake it, then tuck it back in again. This was a difficult task, for her long claws tended to get caught in the loose weave. One time she became so entangled, the sweater having somehow slipped over her head and shoulders, making her look like a bright green and highly agitated ectoplasm, that I had to go to her rescue.

In the evening, after her game with Eric, at that hour when Hansel used to arrive, she continued to go through a period of restless pacing; then she would settle down to putter happily around the house, making alterations we did not always properly appreciate. In her opinion, books were nicer without covers, chairs without seats, and the whole place needed tidying. Whatever was lying around had to be put away, in her treasure chest under my bunk, or disposed of in other ways. Packages of cigarettes were thoroughly shredded, match books chewed up, and everything of Eric's she could lay her hands on had to be laundered.

Although she never did wash her food, we always gave her a pail of water in case she might want to. Mostly she used this as a waste basket, to get rid of anything she didn't like, which included the green corn I brought home one day, thinking to give her a special treat. Also, she enjoyed splashing water all over the floor, probably taking particular delight in making it unpleasant for the cats to walk upon.

Experience had taught me that when she was uncommonly quiet it was time to check on her activities; so one night when she seemed to stay too long hunched over her pail I investigated, and found she had filched a pair of Eric's socks, to give them a thorough drubbing in the pail. After that she became a dedicated washwoman; everything she could find of Eric's—socks, garters, gloves, slippers, shirts snatched off hooks, even sweaters—were gathered up and laundered for him. When she considered them sufficiently clean, she would place them in a sodden heap on the floor to dry.

Always she washed his things, never mine; in her odd little brain these were placed in a different category, and belonged in the treasure chest. Since I am more than somewhat absent-minded, this disposal of my possessions actually turned out to be convenient. No longer did I have to wonder what I had done with my pocketbook, my handkerchief, pen or mittens. I had only to crawl under the bed, and there would be whatever I wanted, in Gretel's heap.

I am a string saver, which means I collect all else I come upon, from rusty nails and bolts to bits of metal, wire, and wood that might come in handy some day, and all of this that will fit goes into my pockets. Therefore I also rather appreciated having my pockets picked, which Gretel did regularly and expertly, slipping her small hand in and withdrawing each item so deftly that sometimes I wasn't even aware of her activity. Such oddments were also carted off to the treasure chest, and again, I found it advantageous to know where a screw or safety pin or paper clip might be found when needed.

But other thievery of hers was less felicitous. When she stole a burning cigarette from the ashtray and hid it with the rest of her booty, some of it highly inflammable, we had to grub wildly under the bed, with Gretel helping amiably by squatting on the pile like a setting hen. Nor did we enjoy having silverware filched from the table, or the coffee pot removed and spirited away before we'd had a chance to sample its contents.

When the confinement time came for Quagga, our oldest female cat, I had doubts about Gretel's views on kittens. Would she consider them akin to mice and suitable for consumption? To be on the safe side we gave Quagga a box in the clothes closet, and tried to remember to close the door while Gretel was indoors. But on the crucial day, somehow it was left open.

Hurrying indoors when I heard a kitten squall, I was horrified to find the bulky Gretel in the box with Quagga. Then, on second glance, I saw with relief that she was doing the kitten no harm, merely helping to wash it dry. This first of Quagga's brood, a blue tiger later named Huckleberry, became from then on Gretel's favorite toy. Time after time he was stolen from Quagga, carried off and tucked in with her other possessions under the bed. When he immediately crawled out she was distressed but not at all discouraged, and hauled him back again, until I took pity on the little thing, put him in the box with Quagga and closed the door. Then Gretel would squat before the door and mourn, in heartbroken trills, until I took pity on her and opened it again.

As Huckleberry grew, he became still more diverting. Instead of merely crawling out of the treasure chest he ran, and after him went Gretel in good-natured pursuit. He was not so swift as she, but always he outwitted her by turning, just when he was about to be caught, to jump over her head. Bewildered, she would look this way and that, and finally discover him bounding off in quite another direction. The more he grew the wilder the chase became, until they thudded through the house like thunder.

They played together, indoors and outdoors, inseparable companions and the best of friends, all through the winter and the following spring, until the very end.

The end came in May, the last part of the month, the twenty-fourth, to be exact, when Gretel must have been one year old almost to the day.

All winter she had accompanied us whenever we went outside, no matter how cold it was. While we shoveled paths she climbed a tree to watch, and when they were finished, she played hide-and-seek with Huckleberry in the maze we had produced, or else had a riotous game with him on the slippery roof. Then she would go to the hole we had chopped in the thick ice over the brook, to paddle in the burning cold water, apparently with no discomfort, and finally return to the house wearing ice bangles on her ankles.

But in May, when the air softened, the trees changed color and showed tiny buds, she refused to go outside. If I tried to pick her up to carry her out, she would slip out of my hands and run almost fearfully to climb to her box on the high shelf. Every animal needs some place of refuge. This was Gretel's. I would not disturb her there, and she knew it.

Perhaps there was some sickness in her. I thought of that, but adhered to the belief that fresh air would cure almost anything. So on that day, the twenty-fourth of May, I lured her with a handful of peanuts and when she came trustingly to get them, seized her and carried her outside.

Near the house was a tall tree that we called her "mad tree." Whenever she was angry she climbed it, sat in a crotch and sulked until our shouted apologies softened her mood and brought her down. Now, eyes blazing, she made for the tree and climbed all the way to the tip of its feather top, indicating she was very angry indeed.

I left her there and after a while came to beg her forgiveness; 67

she turned her back to make it perfectly clear I was still out of favor. I had a dentist's appointment that afternoon which of course had to be kept. But from the set of her body it looked as if she would stay in the tree until I returned. I left without misgivings, and did not worry about her while I was away.

On the way home I stopped in a store to buy cashew nuts for her, and as I approached the house I was smiling, thinking of how her eyes would light up when she sampled this new treat, and how that would make up for the earlier unhappiness.

She was no longer in the mad tree. I went into the house expecting to find her curled up on the bed with Huckleberry, or under it taking an inventory of her treasures, or, still a trifle put out, brooding in her box. She was not in any of these places. Putting some cashews in the box where she would find them when she returned, I called Eric and we went into the woods to search and call, quite confidently at first, then with growing uneasiness and diminishing hope. Finally Eric said, "She might have gone home by herself." At that hour she should have been singing her contented evening song; but we returned to echoing emptiness.

Dinner time came, and passed. After the last light had faded from the sky and the woods were black in a moonless night, a pack of hunting dogs began baying at the foot of the hill. I went out and listened, trying to determine just where they were; but the sound reverberated, seemed to come first from one direction, then from another. Going through dense woods at night is difficult, even with the aid of a flashlight, and haste made me even more clumsy. I had just tripped over a root and lay sprawled on a rock when the baying of the dogs reached a peak of frenzy and suddenly stopped, and I knew they had made their kill.

During the days that followed we continued to search for her, even, in short interludes of optimism, called to her. Almost a week passed before we found all that was left of her in a clump of trampled bushes.

I put away her treasures then, packed in a box. They are still there. Once in a while I take them out to look at them, hold in my hands a moment the buttons and spools, the bits of metal with her teeth marks on them, the favorite hollow bone. Her bed on the high shelf I left just as it was. Sometimes the cats liked to sleep in it.

Eric said the forest must have been aware of our loss, and sent us Joey.

One night my eye was caught by movement in the box where we put food for the birds, and there was Gretel! No, of course not. But the resemblance was striking. I spoke, and the raccoon did not run away. I offered a slice of bread and it was accepted. We seemed to have known each other always.

The next evening the raccoon was not in the box but on our back step, waiting for us, and so it was each evening from then on, until it was the other way around and we were sitting on the back step waiting for her, our pockets full of peanuts. She was a clever little lady who took note of the fact that the upper part of our back door had a pane of glass in it. After we had given her bread and peanuts and gone indoors, she would climb the door to stare at us through the glass, so fixedly and accusingly that we had to go out again, to give her more bread and peanuts.

Eric named her Joey, even though I protested that, resembling Gretel so closely, she had to be a female. This she made a certainty by bringing a baby along one night, and the next night, five babies. Nevertheless, we continued to call her Joey, primarily because she had got used to it and would respond to no other. Soon the babies were named also, and more accurately; Teddybear, Snatcher, Littlest One, Miss Dainty, and Handholder, the last because this fellow liked to put his fingers around one of ours, and hang on.

Now they were all on the back steps every evening, waiting for us to pass out food. Financially this became a serious problem. Finally, after a certain amount of bread and peanuts had been given them, we put down a heap of oatmeal to fill the remaining crevices in their stomachs. They were not too fond of oatmeal, and several of the babies learned to protest by climbing the door as Joey did, to stare at us. The rest made so much noise milling around and squabbling over who had first position in case the door did open, that we had no peace at all until we thought of turning out all our lights. Deducting that we had gone away somewhere, the raccoons would clean up the scorned oatmeal and depart.

After a while I began to notice another raccoon hovering each night in the background, a shadowy figure barely visible under 69 the trees. When Joey and her family left and we went indoors, this raccoon came to snuffle around, hunting for crumbs the others might have left. We felt sorry for her and put another slice of bread on the step, just for her. She repaid us by bringing around babies also, four of them, and we had to dole out still more bread.

The two mother raccoons seemed to respect each other's schedules. The second never came while Joey was still there, and Joey never returned after the other had taken over. But the babies began to get mixed up. Sometimes we counted six or seven in Joey's batch; again, there would be seven or eight in the second shift. Obviously some of the youngsters came in for double portions.

Then one night the four second shift babies were alone. The following night Joey had seven babies in tow, and two others arrived later, again without their mother. The third night Joey had all the babies, and we never again saw the other mother.

Joey was far from pleased. Keeping track of five lively, noisy youngsters had been nerve-wracking. Taking care of nine was enough to drive any mother to distraction. Nevertheless she accepted the orphans and rushed to their rescue whenever danger seemed to threaten. They, in turn, obeyed her faithfully, just as they had their own mother. When a dog barked or something not immediately identifiable rustled in the dark under the trees, or Joey became aware of a lurking presence our senses were too dull to detect, she would stand on her hind legs, sniff, then give an almost inaudible grunt. At once the babies would slip away, soundlessly, not going together but in different directions, and we would hear them scrabbling up trees here and there, seeking safety in the higher branches. Joey would wait, standing guard until she was sure they were all up, then she herself climbed a tree. There she stayed until the menace, whatever it had been, was gone. When she climbed down, head first, that was a signal for the babies. One by one they descended their trees to join her, and all gathered again around the food.

The four orphans were named also: Big Fellow, Dancer, the Timid One, and the last, simply, the Cripple. This one had had a foreleg broken somehow, perhaps in a poorly set trap, and walked with a bad limp.

70

Along with the financial difficulty we had another: getting in and out of doors. Whenever it was absolutely necessary for us to do so, we had to step over raccoons, wade through them, sometimes, if they were too ardently friendly, even carry one or more along, wrapped around our legs. The only way we could travel comfortably and at a fairly reasonable speed was to clear a path by tossing peanuts ahead all along the way. While they stopped to pick up the peanuts we would scuttle to our destination, as fast as possible so the expenditure of nuts would not be too great.

Around the middle of October, Joey, who had grown very fat, stopped visiting us. No doubt she had gone into hibernation early because she had put on enough weight to carry her through the winter. The babies still came nightly but did not linger, and no longer climbed the door to peer through the glass; they had grown too heavy and lethargic.

There is something indescribably pathetic in the appearance of an animal close to hibernation. All joy of living is gone. Movements are slow, listless, indifferent. Even though food is taken from your hand as always and the relationship is just as friendly, you feel the animal withdrawing, setting up a barrier you cannot break through; in an effort to do so you begin to speak louder, as one does to the dying. But saddest of all is the expression in the eyes, an inward-turning, haunted look of termination. So I have come to think of hibernation as "the little death," and sometimes toy with the idea that it might be just as feared as the true end of life.

In the eyes of one after the other of the babies this look came, and each night fewer gathered on the back steps; finally only three, the smallest: the Timid One, the Littlest One, and the Cripple. We knew a trapper had sets in the woods and worried about these three; to prevent them from being lured into the traps and to hasten their hibernation, we gave them all the food they wanted, which was a very great deal.

On the last day of October there was snow. By nightfall about an inch lay on the ground. The three raccoons did not come until quite late, and when they did, let us know by whimpering and scratching at the door, much like dogs. They had that look in their eyes and we knew it was their last visit. We gave them each a slice of bread and held more in readiness, but as soon as they 71 had finished just the one slice they gathered together, gave us a farewell glance over their shoulders and shuffled away through the snow. I like to think they made that one brief visit because they wanted to say goodbye..

Later I followed their tracks in the snow; they went through the woods, far into the woods, to the base of a great old dead tree. There, in its hollow, they slept now, curled up in tight balls, heads tucked under tails, or perhaps with their arms around each other, as Hansel and Gretel had once slept in our house.

From the end of October to the end of May is seven months, and that is a long time in the life of any animal. You could hardly resent being forgotten; indeed, you would expect to be. But one night the following year, just toward the end of May, I went outside for some reason, heard a sudden rustling in old leaves on the ground and saw a large animal come lunging toward me. I caught my breath, then called out a welcome. It was Joey; and running to catch up with her, to greet me also, were some others of the old gang.

A few nights later the rest came. All had survived the winter, even the Cripple; and now everything was as it had been, raccoons paying nightly visits, waiting on the doorstep, squabbling over first position, climbing the door to stare at us, chirring and chuckling, giving us no peace and much pleasure and no end of worry over the grocery bill.

In June, Joey brought five new babies to add to the pleasure and worry, and our family numbered fifteen. By this time news of our wealth had gone abroad, and quite a few people came to view it. The raccoons' reception of these visitors was puzzling. Toward some they showed no sign of mistrust, approached without hesitation to accept peanuts from strange hands, delighted the donors with their antics. Other callers, after waiting hours and hours, had to go away disappointed. As soon as they had left, the raccoons would come swooping in, as if they had been lurking the whole time in the shadows at the edge of the woods, just holding off until the objectionable ones were gone.

Sometimes I knew why the people were objectionable; among them was the woman who brought along her raccoon coat, expecting me to admire it, and another who tried to press on me the gift of a raccoon cap. In others I could discover no fault, but from then on regarded them with suspicion; there must have been something wrong with them.

Fortunately most visitors brought food; otherwise I doubt we could have continued to give satisfactory service. A raccoon stomach seems to be bottomless. A loaf of bread, a pound of peanuts, and still the hands reach up, begging for more. And we wondered about the future. Of the fifteen raccoons, seven were females. If each of these had babies the following spring, say four apiece, and Joey had another four . . . The total we arrived at set us to wracking our brains for ways to make additional money to feed all those mouths.

We needn't have. Nothing was wrong with our mathematics, except that we had left nature out of the reckoning. She took note of a surplus, which she cannot abide, and at once acted with her customary efficiency.

The first raccoon we found a little way back in the woods, lying at the edge of the brook, half in, half out of the water. It was the Littlest One. A few nights later Teddybear came and would not dance for his food as had been his custom, and when we gave him a slice of bread anyway, fingered it mournfully and dropped it. That was the last time we saw him. One by one the others came and did not eat, and disappeared. We wrote to the Conservation Department for information and advice. The reply told us the raccoons undoubtedly had contracted a disease called leptospirosis, highly contagious, epidemic, and swiftly deadly.

So they all left us, all, ironically, but the Cripple. One of nature's rules, which she herself violates only rarely, is that a species must survive; so the Cripple lived on, to keep lonely vigil on our back steps, and finally go limping through the first snow, to curl up in little death in the hollow tree, with no warmth beside her.

Now she, too, is long gone, but her great-grandchildren, or perhaps, more accurately, her great-great-great-great-grandchildren, each summer make the nightly pilgrimage through the woods, along the path of tradition to the house where, ancient legend written on the earth tells them, welcome and food await.

If you have cats, as was only too evident with us, people assume you'd like more. Almost every fall vacationers would leave a parting gift of kittens on our doorstep, or somewhere in the vicinity. They would be of all sizes and colors, but always had one thing in common; they'd be hungry. It seemed unkind to send them on such a long journey with empty stomachs, so we'd give them as much as they wanted to eat, then if there was money enough, take them to the vet; or else, as was most often the case, get out the bottle of chloroform. Older, fully grown cats we usually just ignored, optimistically presuming they belonged elsewhere, had come merely to pay a visit and would go away again, as, indeed, they eventually did—all except one.

Late in the fall, when vacationers had long since departed and snow lay on the ground, we saw this one hanging around near the rabbit cage. From experience I knew that one direct glance from me would be interpreted as a tendering of friendship, so I didn't dare really look at her, but from the corner of my eye I noted she was black and scrawny, sparsely furred and skinny tailed, not at all pretty. Nor, apparently, did she have

charm to make up for her lack of beauty; her manner was furtive, her movements were awkward. It seemed unlikely that she would be cherished by anyone, but I told myself she undoubtedly had a home of sorts somewhere, and if given no encouragement would return there. Our cats did their best to get rid of her. All day they spat and howled, but instead of running off, all she did was crawl under the rabbit cage to hide. When night fell she was still around.

The next morning was blustery and cold; although we knew it to be unwise, we indulged our weakness to the extent of putting out food for her, leftovers our cats had rejected, not calling to her or speaking as we did so, simply placing the dish on the snow and walking away. Hunched up in front of the cage, ready for a quick dash under if need be, she paid no attention. So, we thought, she was not hungry after all. Some time later I glanced out of the window and noticed the plate was empty, but quite possibly our own cats, coming upon the food and deducting it had been put down for the other, took malicious pleasure in gobbling up what previously had been considered unpalatable.

On this second day their belligerence toward the stray increased, now that they knew with certainty that she wouldn't fight back. They'd have had more fun, of course, if she had run from them and they could have chased her through the woods; but even so, they enjoyed making her scuttle back under the rabbit cage every time she dared emerge. Soon a regular path was worn there, from her many comings and goings. Evidently this poor refuge had become home to her and she spent the nights there also. Once when she wasn't around I squatted down to peer under, and saw the round nest she had pressed in the hay fallen from the cage.

We told ourselves it would warm up soon, that lots of cats lived on their own in the woods, that we already had more than enough and she wasn't even attractive. But whenever I went outside and couldn't avoid glancing at her, I could see how she was shivering. We wondered, too, where she was obtaining water, with the ground frozen and the brook covered with ice. But wild animals were faced with the same problem; they ate snow. If she had any sense at all, she would do likewise.

Nevertheless, one night when the wind blew harder than ever, driving snow under the rabbit cage, I stood before it and   75 said, "Oh, all right. Come on, then." Toward these words so grudgingly spoken the miserable black thing came instantly, to creep into my arms; I carried her into the house, past Eric, who shrugged his shoulders but registered approval in eyes that could not lie, past the outraged glare of all the other cats, put her in the bedroom and closed the door.

It wasn't long before the bone fide members of the household turned the intrusion into a diversion. Lined up before the door, they snuffled along the crack and spat taunts, daring the other to come out and face them.

Half an hour later, when I chased them away and went into the bedroom, I found the stray sitting on the lower corner of Eric's bed, still shivering a bit but washing herself ardently, and purring. I said, somewhat idiotically, "Boo!" and she answered with a disarming little "Prrrt?" Now that I looked at her, actually for the first time, I saw she had one redeeming feature. Her eyes, large, round, vivid green in the black setting, were of such compelling depth that, having looked into them, you noticed nothing else. The thin face, gaunt body, straggly fur didn't matter. She had extraordinary beauty, in those eyes.

For five days she stayed on the lower corner of the bed, nowhere else, even though when Eric lay down he patted an invitation for her to join him higher up; this had become her new home. Three times a day I carried her outside to make her contribution to the earth's fertility and get chased under the rabbit cage. I'd wait for a while, call to her, snatch her safely away from the menacing horde, take her back to the bedroom, put her on the lower corner of the bed, and close the door. That was her life, except for the little game we played. Whenever I opened the door I said "Boo," and she answered "Prrt." So, finally, she came to be known as Boo, although later on, more often we called her the Boob; without doubt she was the most stupid, unenterprising cat we'd ever encountered.

She seemed entirely satisfied to remain inactive. Except for the washing, which was her only and almost constant occupation, she did nothing at all but sit quietly on the bed, and might have gone on this way indefinitely, I suppose, if I hadn't decreed otherwise. As long as she had become a member of our family I thought she should join it, and thus free me from the extra chore of fixing a separate plate for her, filling another bowl with water, and carrying her outside. On the sixth day I opened the bedroom door.

The other cats immediately rushed in, took possession of the room, but to their credit, granted her squatter's rights. Just as they had not invaded her retreat under the rabbit cage, so now they did not try to chase her off the corner of the bed. What was hers was hers, little though it might be.

After the door had been open a few days she made a first timid attempt at exploration; she hopped down and stood in the doorway. The others gave her this right also, but every once in a while, in passing, reached out to clout her, just for the devil of it. She never retaliated, only winced and sometimes, if the blow happened to be a hard one, cried out, and kept right on standing there.

That was when we became aware of her stupidity. In size she was a match for any of them. If she had hit back they'd soon have been put in their places and I'd have been spared the trouble of running to her rescue all the time, a thankless task, usually; even in this respect she was dull-witted. I had been good to her: I had fed her well, tended her needs, shown her every kindness. Yet sometimes when I approached she would wince as if she expected me to strike her also, then, if we happened to be outside, turn and run away. This was most annoying, especially if it was raining and I had just bent down to pick her up.

There was also her inability to comprehend the swinging door. It worked either way, quite easily. In varying length of time all the others had learned to use it; so had the raccoons and, to our occasional distraction, wild animals from the woods. But Boo? No. I put her through to show her how it operated and she clutched at me in terror, as if she expected to fall at least seventeen stories on the other side. I held it open for her so she could see it was a means of entrance. She stared at me amiably with those big beautiful vacant eyes and waited for me to pick her up; and like as not when I tried, she would suddenly take fright and run away.

After a long, long time she did come to understand there was some way she could get in or out, but the exact procedure still eluded her; she would try to push against the whole door, or else the wrong panel. By sheer accident she did sometimes find the right one, but such fortuitous experiences did not add up to knowledge.

She also had an odd way with food. When I put down her plate, no matter how hungry she was she wouldn't come at once, but waited until some time after I had left the room to go and eat, as if this were a prohibited action she had to engage in furtively.

A strange, muddle-headed creature she was, with us yet not one of us, like a not very well-known guest paying a visit. Although I fed and cared for her and carted her around, Eric knew her better; she was his cat. You could say she favored him because she shared his bed, but I doubt that was the reason, or the sole reason. Many of the others showed the same preference, bestowing affection on him, regarding me as no more than a servant to take care of their wants, and a boss to be obeyed. I found this not at all disconcerting, and sometimes my apparent indifference would irk Eric. "You don't *need* anyone," he'd complain. He was wrong, of course; I needed them all, most especially Eric himself. But it was sufficient for me that they were, quite simply, there. What I didn't need was to possess. Perhaps a display of possessiveness is required to show love, and my lack of one seemed proof of the other's absence.

Eric was just the opposite, flattered by any display of affection, responding with an abundance of true Viennese sentiment. Because Boo was fond of him, her stupidity, which I found slightly irritating, only made him the more tenderly solicitous. Returning from a shopping trip one day, he handed over two lovely new feeding bowls; one orange in color, the other green. "The red one is for Boo," he said. Hesitating only a moment, I picked the green, which turned out to be correct—in his eyes the orange was brown—and from then on took care to put Boo's food in that bowl; but for Eric, not Boo. To her I gave the same regard as the others, but no special attention.

Then one bright sunny day I was looking out of the window as she crossed the yard; not really watching her, but she happened to be in my line of vision; and because she was, I saw her walk straight into a tree.

Oh, we were stupid, not she! She was blind, and we had been

too blind to notice. Now comprehension came sweeping in. Her slowness to join the family had not been timidity; her unwillingness to fight back had not been cowardice; her inability to use the swinging door had not been lack of comprehension. She did not go to her food immediately because she didn't know it was there; first she had to smell it, then sniff around to determine its exact location. Sometimes she ran away when I tried to pick her up—sometimes, not always—because sometimes I neglected to speak to her, and my footfall, the crunch of gravel, the snapping of a twig made a noise that had what source? She didn't know, and fled.

Now I saw how clever she was, lifting her feet high, as I had learned to do in the dark, putting each pad down carefully, testing the ground for unevenness or obstacles, so that almost never did she run into anything as she had on that sunny day when quite by chance I saw her bump into the tree. She had kept us in the dark for a long time. But once we were aware of hers, we offered a different life.

I carried her out of doors, as I had in the beginning. No more did she have to fear falling down seventeen flights on the other side of the swinging door, or try to discover where it might be. Whenever she started feeling her way cautiously across the room, I cleared a path through the mob of other cats, and soon they came to know she was in some way special, and must no longer be teased. When I served her dinner I let her smell the food first, and always put the bowl down in exactly the same spot. And we tried to take care not to move the furniture about.

This last made her a trifle overconfident. Small chairs do have a way of wandering, and sometimes, in supreme trust, she would leap upon one that wasn't there; then the startled parabola she described in the air was a very funny and terrible thing to see. We, too, moved about; often she would bump into us but at once, with a gesture of grace, this mishap was converted into a caress against our legs.

Outside, beyond our surveillance, she got along well enough. Now that I kept an eye on her I noticed she had by trial and error paced out a safe route to travel. She would start where I had put her down at the foot of the steps, cross the yard, turn to the right when she came to a certain boulder, go toward a large

79

hemlock at the edge of the woods and, amazingly, climb it to the first limb; then, having carefully lowered herself to the ground, she would circle the tree, go through a patch of fern marked by a line of brown from her daily passage, and after that, disappear in the woods. She would not be gone long, no more than fifteen or twenty minutes, and always reappeared at exactly the same spot, just behind the rabbit cage under which she once had lived. She would stop for a moment at the entrance to this old residence, perhaps remembering the misery she had known in it, then go toward the back door, turn and follow the side of the house to reach the front steps. There I picked her up and carried her indoors. Never was there any variation, and every step of her path was known to us, except for the part that went through the woods.

She was happy. Blindness had put her in favor and the inconveniences of it were now taken for granted. All through the summer she enjoyed her small pleasures quietly, gratefully, with no more fear; then came the end, in October, about halfway along her path, where it went through the woods. Did she look like a rabbit?

I don't suppose the hunter wasted any pity on her—she could not have looked like much, lying bony flat, mouth half open in surprise at this thing she had seen in her night—unless he happened to bend down to examine her more closely, and noticed the beauty of those sightless eyes. Going from one darkness to another could not have changed them, not so soon, anyway.

Never did it seem remotely possible that we'd wage war against any animal, but that was how it turned out with Baby Jake. Actually, the battle originated, literally, in Jake, and was instigated, inadvertently, by the raccoons. One thing led to another, which is the way most wars start.

For a while there were just the raccoons, and nightly distribution of rations was at least fairly peaceful; then Jake came horning in, not at all unpleasantly, to be sure, but whenever he arrived, we fled, in a hurry. Although we didn't know him we had heard much about him—all bad—and avoidance seemed advisable; until I began taking pictures. With a camera in my hands I am even more stubborn than a raccoon, which is far more stubborn than the proverbial mule. That was how we finally got acquainted, Jake and I, through the camera's eye, so to speak.

Contrary to what we had been told, he turned out to be a decent fellow. In all the turmoil of shoving, bickering, snatching raccoons, with flash bulbs popping and badly aimed peanuts or chunks of bread sometimes hitting him, he remained courteous. He didn't even take offense when, in backing up to get a shot, I stepped on his tail, nor when I tripped over him in the dark. Fortunately. If he did object to something, the way he expressed his displeasure was overpowering. So admirably did he contain himself that by the time the weather turned cold, I was already beginning to resent hearing a particularly obnoxious person called a skunk.

With the first light snowfall the raccoons got that faraway look in their eyes and whispered away, their fat bottomless bellies close to the ground, to curl up in their winter sleep, and Jake had the field all to himself. That was how we became still better acquainted. Just because the raccoons had departed was no reason why Jake should go hungry, I thought, so I sat on the back steps and chucked out pieces of bread to him. He ate daintily and finally trusted me enough to come snuffling around my feet, with his tail down instead of up and his body going all one way instead of twisted around to threaten me with the weapon he carried under his tail. In other words, we had become friends. Then the snow got deeper and he also stopped coming around.

Such is the inconstancy of humans that we had forgotten about Jake, when one night, early in March, I heard a rustling as I went down the back steps, and saw a skunk dancing around me. The first thing I thought of, a few cases having been reported in the vicinity, was rabies. But as I stood afraid to move, the skunk continued to dip in and out, circling around my feet with no menace but considerable grace and charm; and at last I realized the display was truly a dance, of joyful reunion. Here was my old friend Jake, and he had not forgotten me. Having awakened to greet the spring, he was back, telling me how glad he was to see me; especially since he was very hungry. So we took up where we had left off the previous winter. I sat on the back steps handing out bread; he ate until his stomach, which had a bottom, was full. Then he went quietly away, making a droll tracery of pudgy skunk tracks in the snow.

It was some time before I noticed that the wandering, crisscrossing tracks led invariably to the barn, under which wood rats had tunneled and lived during the winter; and a still longer time before I was aware of the fact that the rats' tunnel had been considerably enlarged. In spite of all I've read, I still remain ill-informed or even misinformed on the habits of wild animals, so I did not know then that where rats go, skunks follow; where rats live, skunks soon take up residence; and where skunks are, rats cease to be. In the eyes of man, this should be one of nature's most fortuitous arrangements.

At last there was no mistaking the fact that Jake had taken over the rats' quarters. A mound of earth two feet high and two feet across appeared at the entrance of the tunnel; also an assortment of dishes the rats had swiped and hidden under the barn. Then things began to disappear: burlap bags, string, a quantity of loose hay, bits of cloth, an old mop, even a piece of vinyl glass.

Here my reading had actually led me astray. All the books I've seen say that skunks don't build their own homes; they bunk in with woodchucks or crawl into abandoned rabbit burrows and are satisfied to leave things as they find them. Well, either the books were wrong or Jake was exceptional. Judging from what appeared and what vanished, he'd obviously done considerable renovating. Once, in one of the dishes he returned, there was even an old, earth-blackened nickel. It pleased me to think of this as a tip for good service.

But toward the middle of May that service began to deteriorate, just as it may in any restaurant grown too popular to give special attention to its steady customers. The snow was gone now and the winds were blowing warmer; the raccoons woke and came back, their bottomless bellies all shrunk from the winter's long fast, and poor Jake, when he came for his evening handout, was shoved aside. On the outskirts of the noisy, snatching horde he hovered, managing to pick up a morsel every now and then, too often only to have it snatched from his very mouth by a robber hand.

Although the provocation was enormous, he refrained from using the weapon under his tail; perhaps because he knew from experience it would have no effect. Like the great horned owl, the raccoon seems to enjoy immunity to the skunk's venom; of all those I have known, Hansel was the only one to show signs of having suffered. However, I felt sorry for Jake, and devised another way to give him his rations. Early in the evening, before the raccoons arrived, I would go to the entrance of his tunnel and call, "Hi, Jake!"

83

Soon a sleepy little black and white head would poke out, mouth open wide enough to please the most exacting dentist; I'd shove a few slices of bread into it, the head and the bread would slowly recede, and that would be that. Jake would be fed.

Sometimes, instead of bread, I'd give him a plate of leftovers. He would take the dish between his teeth, pull it into the tunnel, and a day or two later, evidently when he did his housecleaning, return it to me, all washed and polished.

That was how Jake got twisted around and became a day instead of a night animal. Each evening his stomach seemed to wake up a little earlier. First, on my way from one chore to another, I'd see his head poked out of the tunnel, shiny shoe-button eyes watching every move I made; I would stop whatever I was doing to get him a snack. Then he started standing just in front of the tunnel; and finally, with the sun still shining, he was following me around, frequently accompanied by several of the cats who were also hungry.

The next step came as a matter of course. When I prepared the cats' food, I put a generous portion of it into a separate dish for Jake; and often, with feline perversity, the cats decided to eat with him instead of each other. One, a little female named Spook, particularly enjoyed his company. While Jake followed me, she followed him, her pleasure being to pounce on his lovely feathery tail. As always, Jake was a gentleman. For days and days he allowed this game to be played; until Spook, becoming entirely too careless, raked her sharp claws across the tender part of the skunk's anatomy where the weapon was located. Jake gasped and growled and his reflexes functioned perfectly. Only a small sample of his ire did he give the cat, but it was enough to send her off, straight as an arrow and almost as fast, for a couple of hundred feet before she stopped to consider just what had happened to her. For a while, to the particular distress of Eric, whose nostrils were more sensitive than mine, the air around our house smoldered, until Spook with desperate tongue washed away the stench of her misadventure. If she had been a dog, Eric would have suffered for weeks; the cat is lucky enough to have saliva that speedily does away with odor. Nevertheless, from then on Spook found it preferable to play with ordinary cats' tails, even her own if no other happened to be available.

Toward the end of May, Jake began to act peculiar, even

downright unfriendly. He stopped following me, at feeding time he would just barely stick his head out of the tunnel, grab the plate of food with a whuffing sound close to a snarl and drag it inside, so that I could no longer watch him eat, and the cats dared not keep him company.

Next we began hearing peculiar noises under the barn, small cries like tiny animals being done to death. We would pound on the wall and at once the noise would stop, only to start up again after a short silence. This reassured us somewhat, for an animal in agony does not cease wailing simply to listen to someone pounding on a wall. But what was the explanation? Did the crying have something to do with Jake?

In a few days we came to realize it reached a crescendo just after Jake had hauled the plate into his tunnel; and a few days after that we found out what it was. When I took out Jake's supper and called at the entrance of the tunnel as usual, a head appeared as usual—but not Jake's. This was a bright, new pert, tiny replica of Jake's. He had become a mother!

The little head remained visible for only an instant before it was jerked back into the tunnel, to be replaced immediately by Jake's, wearing a most unfriendly expression. First she snarled into the tunnel, then she snarled at me; then she took the plate between her teeth and dragged it inside. At once the noises began; not cries of distress at all, but squeals of baby skunks squabbling over the food.

The next day and the next, in fact so many days that I began to believe I must have imagined I saw the little one, no other head than Jake's appeared in her doorway. But finally, just as she was picking up the plate one evening, she got a nudge from behind that dunked her nose into the food, then seemed to go through a strange upheaval, and two tiny skunks wormed out from under her belly. She snarled and poked them back with her nose, but as soon as she turned they were out again. At last she gave up and allowed them to go to the plate, where they nuzzled at the food and squealed. However, Jake made it clear that my presence was unwanted by twisting her rear around to show me the weapon; I took the hint and left, and when I returned later, all three of them were gone, and so was the plate. And underneath the barn all was quiet.

When I called the following evening, Jake and the two babies appeared at once; then another little head emerged, and another, and another, until there were six. And what a gathering that was around the food plate, what a chorus of cries, what a lovely shifting design of black and white as they changed places to hunt for choice morsels!

From that time on my presense was tolerated. Jake no longer threatened me, the babies gave me the complete trust common in all infancy. Sometimes when I called, Jake allowed, or perhaps was forced to allow the babies to precede her. When they took meat from my hand she observed, and took some also. When they crawled without fear on my lap, she ventured there also. But when they let me stroke them she watched dubiously, and ducked as the hand was slipped over her back. She would not go so far.

This was the nicest time for all of us, I think; the babies were still dependent, their world no larger than the area under the barn and a few feet beyond, so secure that neither Jake in her nocturnal wandering nor I in the safety of my own house needed to have the slightest worry about them. Oddly enough, Jake herself brought an end to the ideal existence. One day—the sun was still quite high—I caught a glimpse of her bustling down the hill, and just behind her, bustling along in exactly the same way, were two of the babies, one on each side, so close that their noses were tucked into the fur on her haunches. I called out, but that only increased their speed away from me.

A short while later the same scene was repeated, and still later, once again; I knew what it meant. Jake had moved her babies, making three trips down the hill, taking them by twos. That night no one came out of the tunnel when I called, and Jake's food remained untouched until after dark, when the raccoons found and dug their greedy little fingers into it. I was hurt. Had I not provided a good home for Jake, although inadvertently, and fed her well? And I was disappointed; I had planned to take pictures and had delayed. Now it was too late.

But no, I was wrong. The following day, at about the same time, I witnessed the same scene as the day before, only in reverse; Jake and two of her babies came trudging up the hill. They went directly to the barn and into their tunnel, and a few moments later Jake emerged alone. I watched her go down the hill and disappear in the woods, and after quite a long wait saw her return with two more babies. Into the tunnel they went, and again Jake came out alone to make a third trip for the last two of her family.

This set me to thinking; how did the babies know they were to go two by two; how was it established which two were to go; how did those that were left know they must stay where they were until Jake returned? And most puzzling of all, how did those that had been delivered into the tunnel know they should stay there and not follow their mother down the hill again?

These questions were never answered, but I saw the performance often enough. Sometimes Jake and her babies were at home under the barn, sometimes they would be away for a day, or two, or three. I stopped worrying about them; clearly Jake knew what she was doing. But I was curious. One day when I saw a hurrying threesome start down the hill, I followed at a discreet distance.

In the very beginning, when our house was creaking new and our land still unexplored, I had gone for a walk in the woods and coming to the foot of this hill, had suddenly lost my footing and fallen. The reason for my imbalance was that one leg had gone down into a hole, which I had not seen because it was covered with leaves. Investigation led to the discovery of three holes, rather widely separated, two invisible under a blanket of old leaves, the third open and evidently recently enlarged.

Here, once, when the land below had been pasture, a woodchuck had lived; now the abandoned pasture had grown to brush, making the habitat unsuitable for woodchucks. Yet the underground chamber was occupied. By what? I kept my eye on the burrow and finally determined foxes had taken residence there; then, when they left or perhaps were dispossessed, a wildcat moved in, and stayed for two years. After his departure the burrow remained vacant for quite a while, perhaps because traces of his menacing scent lingered. But now one of the entrances had been cleared again, just enough to permit the passage of one small skunk and her six babies, and into it Jake and the two youngsters disappeared.

Wise Jake! From here she could take them foraging in the woods, teach them how to dig up grubs, catch snakes, hunt mice 87

and rats. Living under the barn they would be forever dependent upon us and our bounty, and somehow she knew that the
human hand, however kindly and lavish, was impermanent
and therefore an untrustworthy source of sustenance. She put
her trust in nature, which offered hardship and danger, but was
eternal.

Ironically, it was nature that brought tragedy to the little
family.

For three days it rained. These three days Jake and her babies
stayed away. I thought they must be quite safe and snug in their
house in the woods, and was not concerned. Then on the fourth
day there was a steady downpour, all day long. The brook, usually no more than a meekly chuckling glitter in the sunlight,
easily forded here and there on stepping stones, became a roaring torrent, hurling away the stepping stones, crashing against
larger boulders to toss spray high in the rain-soaked air. In the
afternoon it began to overflow its banks. Runnels of water
trickled down the hill, increased in size to become small streams,
merged to form larger streams. Here and there the white head
of a miniature waterfall appeared.

Gazing out of the window on this wild scene, suddenly I
caught sight of Jake toiling up the hill, all six babies with her
this time, lined up behind her. No doubt she was trying to take
them to higher ground because their home down below was
flooded. Her movements were uncertain and jerky; she went
here, there, running swiftly, backtracking when she came to
high water, making wide detours to avoid newly created streams,
but always turning again to try to go higher. Whichever way
she went the six babies followed, copying each of her movements
with precision. They looked so frightened, so wet and muddy
and bedraggled, that I called Eric and we went out in the rain
to get ourselves all wet and muddy and bedraggled in an effort
to help them.

While Jake tried one fording place after another, finding each
under deep water, we slogged around testing and discarding
lumber until we came upon two boards that we thought were
wide enough to be safe and long enough to bridge the brook.
Carrying these to a section where the banks were high and level,
we placed them side by side, their ends resting on the banks.

Underneath, the water boiled, making me dizzy when I walked across, but the bridge seemed sturdy enough, and I returned to the house to get a handful of meat, which Jake loved and apparently could smell a mile against the wind. Two little balls of it I put on the far bank, close to the bridge; the rest was placed on the bridge itself, in small portions about a foot apart. Then we stood back to watch.

While we had been working, Jake had gone downstream and was now on her way up again, in desperation jumping over the smaller tributaries, with all the babies behind her jumping over them in turn. When she came to what had been a fording place she would go close to the water and dip her paws in, searching for the way to cross. The babies would go close to dip their paws in also, and she would seize the nearest one, take its whole head in her mouth to drag it away. After that she would cuff them all, drive them back, and the trek upstream would begin again.

Finally they reached our bridge. Jake sniffed at the meat and turned away, each of the babies sniffed and turned. She put her two front paws on the bridge, hesitated, then crawled onto it; one of the babies crawled on just behind her. She took a few steps, came to another ball of meat and passed it. The baby behind her followed close, and others began to climb on the bridge.

We held our breaths; it looked as though our scheme was going to work. Then Jake caught sight of us. She stared, turned to look back at her babies, in sudden panic drove them off the bridge and scrambled off herself. In this strange, hostile world we ourselves had become strangers to her. If she could no longer trust the very ground on which she had walked safely for so long, could we not have changed and become untrustworthy also?

We took a last look at the seven of them milling around and went back to the house. But after I had dripped a fair-sized pool on the floor next to the stove, I went out again. Jake was near the entrance to her tunnel under the barn, and five of the babies were with her. I gave them a chunk of meat and went up to the bridge to search, but there was no trace of the sixth baby. I suppose by that time its body had been washed far downstream.

From then on the family stayed around the barn, until the middle of summer, when it began to split up. Sometimes Jake would come to dinner with only two babies, sometimes all five babies would be there, but not Jake. Occasionally I would see the young ones out foraging on their own, or going down the hill to their other residence, and Jake coming along in the opposite direction. They would greet each other, then continue on their separate ways.

When the nights turned cold I saw less and less of them, often was not sure which I did see. Finally there was only a single one, always the same. He came to dinner regularly, and the first snow told us he had taken over the old family home under the barn. Somewhere in the woods, perhaps down in the old woodchuck hole, the rest of them slept, rousing on warmer nights to do a little hunting, but spending most of the winter in semi-hibernation. Not so with Baby Jake. He remained active all through the winter, and my relationship with him became much as it had been with Jake; I would go to the tunnel and call, a sleepy head would emerge and graciously accept the food I offered.

Life for him was truly ideal, and I was pleased. There is nothing more gratifying than knowing that, in providing for another creature, no matter how insignificant, one has attained perfection. Baby Jake had a warm dry house, plenty of bedding—I would put an armful of hay near his door and was amused to watch it gradually disappear; he had regular meals and moreover, food of excellent quality. Now that there was only the one mouth to feed, we could afford to give him what he liked best, raw meat.

It was, in fact, too good a life to last. One exceptionally warm night when the air smelled of spring, I went outside, heard something rustle toward me, and there was Jake at my feet, bowing and dipping in her dance of reunion. I gave her food, she ate and departed. The next night, at about the same time, I heard a sudden commotion that sounded like a pack of rats murdering each other, coming from the vicinity of the barn; just as I arrived there, out of the tunnel shot Baby Jake, and after him, in a nauseating wave, a great stench that rose and spread, swiftly engulfing the barn and me and the surrounding territory. And following that came Jake.

What had happened was clear enough. Jake had returned to her summer home. After having occupied it in great style all winter, Baby Jake had been dispossessed. That night, miserable and stinking, he wandered around forlornly, and where he found a place to retire before morning we did not know. But in the evening he appeared for dinner as usual, looking smug, and seemed so satisfied with life that he didn't even mind sharing his food with the recently returned Jake.

The following morning we saw the reason for his contentment. At the side of our house was a large mound of earth, and under the field stone foundation, a newly dug tunnel. Baby Jake had found even better quarters than the old home under the barn.

Having a skunk living in the apartment below would be quite all right, I suppose, if he were a nice, quiet, well-behaved gentleman. Indeed, Baby Jake was a gentleman, but unfortunately a convivial one. He liked to invite friends in of an evening, and throw a really big party every once in a while; and whoever passed the word around that skunks are practically voiceless certainly never has had one for a neighbor. Their gabbling would wake us in the middle of the night, we'd pound on the floor with the heel of a shoe, for a minute all would be quiet, then it would start up again, no more than a murmur at first, but gradually increasing in volume. Moreover, all too often the party would end up, like so many others, in a fight, and the smell of their disagreement would seep up through the floor boards; then, along with Baby Jake's departing guests, we also had to vacate the building.

That was when the war broke out. During the day we would spend up to an hour carting stones to plug up Baby Jake's tunnel. During the night he would spend perhaps a couple of hours digging a new one, no doubt aided by his friends; and when it was finished, like as not he'd reward them by tossing another party which more often than not would end up in another fight.

We suspected we were losing the war, were certain of it after we had gone once around the house plugging tunnels and there seemed to be no place left to dig, only to have him mock our labor by tunneling under the very boulders we had used as plugs. This, we knew, could go on indefinitely, unless we were lucky enough to strike hardpan somewhere not too close to China.

Meanwhile Jake had had a new litter of young ones under the

barn; soon they would be coming out with her to gather around the dinner plate. Where, we wondered, would they decide to live when they grew up. "Probably in the house," Eric said with a touch of bitterness. He truly suffered; I didn't, so much.

Once I talked with an old trapper who said that after a while you got to like the smell. That, I thought, was impossible; Yet the time came when I searched the wind to find some trace of the odor that had become for me, as for the trapper, "a little like perfume. Strong, sure. But so is perfume, you use enough."

We did not win our war. However, nature stepped in to wage another of her own, and she was ruthless. A second epidemic of leptospirosis swept through the woods and all the skunks succumbed: Jake and her new litter, Baby Jake, and every one of his friends. After that I never saw or even caught a distant whiff of a skunk until this spring, when three orphans were brought to me.

These three seldom smell, only when the raccoon plays too rough and bowls them over; then I wish I could talk again to the old trapper, now long gone, to tell him, "You were right. I have come to rather like that perfume too." Matter of fact, I prefer it to the kind favored by most women, which truly makes me quite ill.

Years ago I started putting a plate of food outside, "for Whoever," I told Eric. During the summer we had no way of identifying Whoever, although we could deduct with fair certainty that the raccoons most often got the food; but when snow fell there were many stories written in it; tracks to tell us Whoever was a homeless cat, a foraging dog, a misplaced opossum, an unlucky raccoon or skunk that hadn't put on enough fat to doze comfortably through the winter, a colony of deer mice or wood rats, or early rising squirrels and birds. However, sometimes a portion of the food disappeared and in the snow around the plate there would be no tracks at all, not even the miniscule indentations of the deer mice.

This mystery might have remained unsolved if I hadn't been outside so much, and if association with animals hadn't endowed me with one of their own traits, the ability to remain immobile over a considerable period of time. Sitting on the steps one fall night, listening to the whisper of comings and goings in the woods, wondering whether a closer footfall, just beyond the pool cast by the back-door light, might be a skunk or a raccoon arriving, I became aware of a flicker of movement near the plate   93 of food. I turned only my eyes, but this was sufficient warning; whatever had been there was gone, and did not return.

The next night again there was that hint of movement, and color: light gray or buff? I couldn't be sure. In fact I wasn't absolutely certain I had seen anything at all. Then, from the corner of my eye, I caught another glimpse of darting color, this time higher up, near the box in the hemlock where we put food for the birds. Nothing frightens animals quite so much as a steady stare; I didn't dare look directly, but fortunately we humans have excellent peripheral vision. So I saw one of the loveliest creatures in the whole forest, a flying squirrel. To give me a good view, the little fellow remained still for a moment, perched on the edge of the box; a small body clothed in tawny silk velvet, a round pixie head with small ears and great dark eyes, a broad flat tail delicate as a feather and, from wrist to ankle, soft skin edged with black folded against its sides.

Rarely is the flying squirrel seen, not because he actually is rare—he lives in tree-top hollows all over America—but because he is so uncompromisingly nocturnal, and so swift of movement. He does not really fly; he glides. He can twist, turn and bank, the flat tail acting as rudder and brake, but his course in the glide is always downward, except for an upward thrust at the end of his journey, which enables him to light on the trunk of a tree. Having done so, he will scamper to the top of this tree, take off again to light on still another trunk, and so make his way along an aerial pathway with hardly any need to come to earth, where most predators lurk.

Now, I realized, I had lured this one into great danger; he could not resist sampling the food I had put down for Whoever. Hunger was stronger than fear. To feed him more safely, from then on I put raw peanuts in the bird box, just at dusk, after the birds had retired, and each night I stood watching while he flicked in and out, so quickly that he was almost invisible, to carry them away. That was how I finally discovered he was not one, but several; he had no more than left the box before he was back again, then I began to see him in several different places at the same time, on a limb of the tree, coming down the trunk, and also in the box. Four I counted, and five, and six.

Once they had got used to me standing there, as much a part

of the night as a tree, they would come scrambling down the hemlock to stare at me curiously; then one by one, never colliding, never disputing, float light as thistledown into the box and out and up, and perched on various branches above, they would fill the night with remote sounds of crackling, and bits of shell would fall like raindrops around me.

I searched and found the place where they lived, a hollow that had been the home of a woodpecker, in a dead maple across the brook. I saw how they came to the feeding station, each evening along the same route, and it seemed they must be quite safe up there, high among the branches. But wherever there is movement in the forest, eyes are watching, and wherever there is life, death waits. It caught the squirrels at the feeding box; a cat, thin, black, silent. He would climb to a branch of the tree above the box and wait, and at that one instant when a squirrel was motionless, pausing to pick up a nut, then and not a split second sooner or later, he would drop down. There would be the thud of his body on the box, a minute squeak of surprise, the clatter of the nut as it fell to the ground, then silence, with the stars still laughing in the sky as if nothing had happened at all.

So they went, one after the other. I felt no bitterness toward the cat, owned by a neighbor who expected him to live on nothing but milk. He needed meat, searched it out, and once he had perfected his canny system, found easy prey.

At last only one squirrel was left. He was either luckier than the others, or cleverer. Night after night he eluded the cat until discouragement drove the poor beast to hunt elsewhere. Then came a time of delight for both of us, the last of the squirrels and me. Perhaps because he was lonely, he adopted me as a playmate.

When I came to stand at the foot of the hemlock he would emit a tiny "Chip-chip," scramble down the trunk, past the feeding box, past my outstretched hand offering a nut, his evident purpose being to fling himself straight into my face; but just short of it he would stop, his twitching nose almost touching mine, his black eyes full of bright mischief, to say, "Chuck!" Then whisk, he was gone. Where? Nowhere. Like the conjurer's wafted kerchief, he had disappeared. A moment later I would catch sight of him again, popping his head around the trunk higher up, this side, that side, playing peek-a-boo. I'd offer the nut again. Sometimes he took it, sometimes instead played another of his games, slipping past the nut to nibble impudently on my fingers.

We were very good friends. Then one night I waited and he did not come, and in the morning the nuts I had left in the box were still there. It was the same the next night and the next. For a few weeks I still made sure I had nuts in my pocket before I went out at night; after that I stopped torturing myself with disappointment and didn't even glance toward the hemlock. So when I passed under the tree one evening and heard overhead that joyous sound, "Chuck, chuck, chuck," I could hardly believe in it. But yes, there he was, back again, still my friend, only in a strange mood.

Ignoring the nuts I hastily put in the box, he flicked down the tree to stare in my face, was away again, high up in the branches to chatter excitedly, then down again. Some time passed before I discovered the reason for his strange behavior. He was not alone; above was another squirrel, gazing at me dubiously. During those weeks he had been gone he must have searched for and found a mate, and now he was introducing her to the feeding box, and to me.

She was properly mistrustful. Night after night he danced up and down the tree to convince her the passage was safe, carried nuts to show her what bounty was below, but she would not join him there. Instead of peanuts, I offered pecans, and such a rare treat could not be resisted. Soon she was coming to pick up nuts as he did, but always following him and imitating his every movement. At last, having watched at a distance the games he played with me, she dared to join in. Then what a merry time we had, the three of us, as they chased up and down and around the tree, playing pranks first on me and then on each other.

All through the winter we met, but when April brought mildness in the air our games came to an end. One squirrel disappeared, the other was preoccupied and always in a hurry, seizing the nut I offered and going immediately, over his bridge of branches and away. I began to feel foolish, standing there slapping at mosquitoes, acting as no more than a vending machine; finally I just put a pile of nuts in the box and stayed indoors.

The nights grew warm. Peepers started croaking in the swamp down the hill. In the woods, dry leaves rustled almost constantly with the passage of awakened life. Soon the raccoons and skunks would be back, demanding handouts, and in no time the raccoons would find the supply of nuts in the bird box. I doubled the nightly ration, so the squirrels would have enough to tide them over the summer. Then one night, as I was putting the nuts in the box, I heard it again, "Chuck!"

There he was, there she was, and both were ready for play. Coming headlong down the tree, he seized the nut I held out, flung it away with a devil-may-care flourish and nibbled delicately on my thumb. She followed, stared at me mischievously, was on my arm and off before I had time to be aware of the almost weightless touch of her body.

Oh, they were nimble, they were merry, and they were many! Here were the two I knew—here and there and here again—and there was another, another, and another, smaller, brighter looking, the young my friends had raised. They came to look me over gravely and, in a sudden dance, flicked lightly over my outstretched hand. They were too young to know I might be an enemy. Very politely, as if conferring an honor, they took the nuts I offered, nibbled busily on the ends a moment, and tossed them away. They were also too young to know hunger, or how the barren winds of winter always follow summer's gentle sighing through the leaves.

They were as difficult to count as fireflies flashing on and off. Was that one on the branch the same I had seen a moment ago, or another? No, now there were two; but was one the same or were they both different? Suddenly these disappeared, and almost simultaneously three appeared on the branch farther out. But which three?

I was at last satisfied with having counted up to eight. Leaving a heap of nuts on the box, I went into the house, evidently with some of the sparkle in their eyes still reflected in mine. Looking up from his typewriter, Eric said rather wistfully, "I wish I could be that happy."

"We are very wealthy," I told him. "The squirrels have babies."

There followed many nights of play and growing friendship; then one day as I walked through the woodlot I saw on the ground the first small ball of fur and bone. I picked it up and held 97 it in my hand, told myself it could be almost anything. But that night I became aware of something I had not noticed before: how the squirrels, in the middle of a game, would suddenly flatten themselves against the trunk of the tree and gaze apprehensively upward. I could detect no change in the night, no sound or movement anywhere between us and the stars; but they were aware of danger, and tried to make themselves invisible.

I found more balls, grew adept at determining what they once had been. This, a wood rat; that, a mouse. And this—one of my friends. Then one night I was present to witness the conversion. I had just left the house, was walking toward the feeding box, my pocket full of nuts; on the box a squirrel sat waiting for me, his little fists curled against his white breast. I spoke to him; he answered with a merry tail-flicking dance. Perhaps if I had not caught his attention he would have been more wary. Suddenly there was swift movement in the air, something as tawny as the squirrels swept across the dark sky with the precision and silence of a cat leaping—in that eyeblink of time I thought with astonishment that somehow a cat had learned to fly—and the next instant there was the pounce of a body on the box. Then there was nothing left for me to look at but the empty box. The owl was gone as silently as it had come. The squirrel was gone as silently at it had died. And something in my heart that had just been laughing was gone, too.

The next day I started making the cage. There is much to be said for freedom, but security has advantages also; in the life of an animal, the two cannot coexist. For the squirrels, I had the power to choose one or the other. For myself there was a choice also; to trap them and see their merriment constricted by wire, or leave them free and watch them die. It was a hard decision to make.

The cage was three feet tall, two feet square, not nearly big enough, but we were in one of our pancake periods; there was no money to buy more. I searched through the woods until I found a good log, split it in half, hollowed out the two sections, fastened them together again with wire and cut out four small doorways, just big enough for a walnut to pass through. I stuffed the log with shredded tissue, dry leaves and soft hay, fastened it near the top of the cage, added a few branches of the tree they knew so well for perches, put a water dish and some nuts on a metal tray down below; then everything was ready and I set the trap on the feeding box.

It was so easy that it hurt. I didn't stay near the tree or call to them, not wanting to give fate any sort of a nudge. Yet even before I had returned to the house I heard the snick of the trap closing.

In it was the little female, the mother. I took her to the porch where I had placed the cage, opened the trap and held it against the door of the cage. She went from one to the other without hesitation, climbed straight up to the log house, slipped through one of the round holes, and I saw no more of her.

The following night I caught my old friend, her mate. He, too, went obediently into the cage, up to the log house and entered. I held my breath. Chipmunks, red squirrels, any number of other animals would not live together peaceably in such close quarters. Would there soon be cries of alarm and anger predicting the death of one or the other if I did not release them? There was a gentle rustling of dry leaves inside the house, then silence.

Each night I put out the trap. Either the family had been larger than I had thought, or other flying squirrels were in the vicinity; the trap clicked shut four more times. After that it remained open and the bait inside untouched until a diminutive deer mouse imprisoned himself, ate without perturbation and when satiated, calmly crawled through the bars.

Five of the squirrels lived placidly inside the log house. The sixth, the last one trapped, was smaller, perhaps of a more recent litter, or from another clan; he was found unacceptable. The others did not harrass him in any way or try to chase him away from the food. They simply ignored him. But when he tried to enter the log house to sleep, they pushed him out. Time after time he poked his head through one after the other of the four doorways, and was told at each to go away. So he perched like a bird on a branch just outside the house from which he was banned, his fists pressed against his breast, his head tucked between them, his feathery tail curled over his eyes. In his sleep he swayed, and sometimes he fell off the branch.

When it seemed he was to remain an outcast I took pity on him and made another small house, which I fastened to his perch. He accepted it gratefully and spent most of the first night happily arranging the bedding to his liking. The others did not show resentment, and respected his title to this annex; from then on there was contentment in the squirrel cage.

But, just as when the chipmunks had been quartered on this same porch, I was not content. The first thought of the squirrels on awakening was not, as with most animals, food, but play; it was almost painful to watch the six of them tumbling about in such a small cage, going through amazing contortions to keep out of each other's way, but sometimes colliding anyway and falling to the floor with sharp squeaks of dismay.

We talked it over and agreed we might try letting them out at night. When the door to the house was closed at the end of the day, the cats counted to make sure no one of them remained hidden in some corner of the porch, I went out and opened the cage.

At first we were disappointed. Only two squirrels ventured out and they did not go far. But gradually they adjusted their mild little selves to this freedom and grew bolder; a new life began for them—and the cats. As soon as the smoky hue of dusk came, the squirrels slipped out of their log houses, but now, instead of beginning to play immediately, they sat on their perches, grooming themselves, one scrubbing a tail draped over his arm, another washing his face with quick strokes of both paws, others scratching meditatively or smoothing down sleep-rumpled fur, until a certain hour, the hour, when they started hopping with excitement, going down often to press their tiny paws against the door of the cage. And at this same hour, the cats lined up on the window seat looking out on the porch, eyes fever bright, tails twitching, waiting for the show to begin. This was the hour for me to open the cage.

The moment I did, squirrels tumbled out like children just released from school, one off in this direction, two in that; in a twinkling they were all over the porch, tightrope walking along the back of a deck chair, scrabbling upside down on the ceiling beams, rattling across the screens, flying the length of the porch to land on the floor with froglike plops. The cats, whimpering with delight, turned their heads in unison like spectators at a tennis match. For hours, while the squirrels played, they hardly moved, except for the head-turning and an occasional rearrangement of the lineup when one, leaning over to get a better view, nudged another off the seat; at once the deposed cat climbed back up, and already preoccupied with watching, squeezed himself in to become part of the audience again.

This was their nightly pastime all through the winter, with special entertainment for Christmas. After having awakened on a previous Christmas morning to find the tree toppled, ornaments scattered, tinsel snaking all over the floor, bulbs broken, and wire chewed, we had decided to put temptation out of the cats' reach by placing our tree on the porch, just in front of the window so we could still enjoy viewing it. Now the squirrels enjoyed it, at closer range, scampering up its trunk, chasing each other over and among the branches, in and out, up and down, fingering the bright ornaments to make them bobble and spin, chuckling with glee. The mound of white stuff that looked so much like snow at the tree's base they found acceptable for bedding, tore off shreds to stuff into their mouths and carry back to the cage. When the big log house and the little outcast's hut were packed so full that they had difficulty squeezing in, sometimes having to pause halfway, with back legs and tail hanging out ludicrously until a passage was cleared, they began making small auxiliary nests in corners of the porch just under the eaves, for what purpose we didn't know. Each morning when I checked before letting the cats out, I found all the squirrels had returned to the cage.

Not until the middle of March did we discover the reason for these other nests. The outcast was the first to be dispossessed. One morning I found him swaying on a branch, drunk with sleep, just as in the days before he was given the hut. All winter his right to it had not been disputed; now whenever he tried to enter another squirrel head popped out and with a sharp squeak that must have been authoritative even though lacking in volume, told him to go away.

A few days later he was joined by another squirrel; then inspection one morning revealed that three of them had not gone back to the cage, but were sleeping absurdly, uncomfortably, in the makeshift nests tucked in corners under the eaves. I persuaded them to return to the cage, but they would not enter either of the houses. From inside the log at the top came sounds of mild bickering; and suddenly I knew how stupid we had been. It was time for their young to be born, for the males to stay away. And they had no place to go. We'd have to release them, I told Eric. But how long would they survive out of doors, after winter-long security had made them fearless?

Sometimes, by whim, fate is kind. The very next morning Eric brought home the mail, a few letters stuffed in his pocket but one held in his hand, indicating it had special importance. With a flourish he took out a check; he had sold a book.

For years we had planned on, hoped for and despaired of adding another room to the house, needed rather desperately because every time Eric carried something to the dump, I hauled it back in again. He could have lived, as before my days with him he had lived, in a suitcase. Given only a few months, I could have packed to overflowing a twenty-one room house.

"Now," Eric said, "which would you rather have, the extra room, or a cage outdoors for the squirrels?"

"The cage for the squirrels," I answered instantly, and he grinned.

"I thought that was what it would be."

We went out at once to search for a fairly level spot clear of trees, found one just in back of the house, measured, added, multiplied, arrived at a total of two-by-fours and wire, and telephoned our order. When you have money, the solution to almost any problem is as simple as that.

But on the day the supplies arrived, so did another letter requesting Eric's presence in New York. It was almost always that way; whenever there was some crisis, or a big job to be done, he was absent. This time, however, I was secretly relieved. Once Eric had decided to make a dog house for Muff, had worked on it ardently for days and days, then when he said it was finished and stood back to admire his handiwork, Muff accidentally leaned against one side, and the whole thing fell apart. He was, as they say in these mountains, no mechanic; while I, to make things even, displayed a most unfeminine proficiency with tools. I knew the cage would really stand if I built it alone.

Perhaps to punish me for this conceit, the weather turned bad as soon as Eric left. Wet snow fell the day I laid the foundation; a howling wind blew when I put up the frame. Perched on swaying roof beams, I rediscovered my fear of height and stayed doubled over, clutching a two-by-four, most of the afternoon, until the even more distressing discovery that I had no handkerchief in my pocket drove me down. The day I tacked on the wire we had an ice storm: steady, almost solid rain fell, coating lumber, wire, staples, hammer, everything but me, with thick ice. But whenever I went indoors tempted to quit, I saw those three male squirrels huddled on their branch, and had to go out again.

Ironically, as soon as the work was finished the weather turned benign, the wind calmed and the sun shone. There was the cage, ten feet long, ten feet high, big enough for a squirrel to take quite a long glide. Under the wood floor was another of wire mesh, to keep out the rats. It had wire sides and a wire roof, so that in winter, snow might sift down to provide the occupants with necessary moisture when the water in their bowl froze.

This bowl I had placed on a shelf just under the roof; even after months of no fear of predators, the squirrels did not like to stay long on the ground. Also high up, at the far end of the cage, were two long log houses, hollowed out as the first had been, but with partitions dividing them into individual dwellings, four in each log, eight in all, each with a private entrance. Here the squirrels could be secluded if they wished. But down below was another long, low building with only one entrance, where they could foregather, should that be their preference; in time this came to be called the community hall. And just in front of its door was their feeding dish.

Some of the supports for the roof were trunks of trees instead of two-by-fours, with branches left on them where squirrels might sit and eat, or groom themselves, or gaze at the world outside; and as a final touch, at the very end, I added branches fresh cut from their favorite trees, hemlock and maple. I looked forward to the grand opening that evening with considerable pleasure; but when the squirrels were moved, cage and all, and their prison door was opened, nothing happened, nothing at all. For hours I hung around, and not a squirrel stirred. The males had squeezed themselves into a small space behind the log house and would not move even when I prodded them with a finger thrust through the wire. Inside the log house, the females were silent. The mound of food, bananas, apples, almonds, pecans, 103 grapes, all the things they liked particularly, remained untouched.

The next day I passed the cage often, each time pausing to glance in. No food had been taken, nothing had changed. But that night, when I entered to put fresh water in their bowl, a wisp of cotton came floating down from one of the big log houses. I stood under it and called, and in a moment a head popped out of a doorway to give me a tilted glance of one part mistrust and two parts mischief, then popped out of sight again.

Some time during the evening they must have moved. I tapped against their old cage, heard not even a faint rustle, took off the top, put my ear against the log house, tapped against it, then lifted it out and pried it open. Somehow I was embarrassed, as if I might be going through someone else's desk drawer, or reading another's letter. Here, all through the past winter, the squirrels had lived. Along the walls, nut kernels were lined up in neat rows. The rest of the log was stuffed with clean shredded cotton, and in it were three small equidistant hollows, the nests of the females.

While I was touching and examining, I had a feeling of being watched; looking up, I saw six squirrel heads poked out of six doorways, peering down at me. I blinked my eyes, and saw only six empty doorways. But at least I had had a glimpse of all of them, had seen, too, a flicker of the old merriment in their eyes. When I left the cage I was grinning foolishly, with pleasure quite out of proportion to anything but the sum of money we had spent to make six small squirrels happy.

A few days later their family was enlarged. Cricket caught a mouse and, being a proper cat, turned it over to me; a very tiny mouse with large ears, big black eyes, almost invisible twitching whiskers and diminutive snowflake feet, a deer mouse, unhurt except for a dent in its tail.

I didn't know what to do with it. Wherever I went, Cricket followed persistently, waiting for me to put it down, so she could catch it again; if she brought me a paper ball, didn't I throw it for her to do just that? At last I took the mouse into the squirrel cage. On my open hand it sat for a moment looking around dazedly, then dropped to the floor, drifted over to one of the tree trunks and disappeared. After a moment I caught sight of it at the top of the trunk, turning sensitive nose this way and that to test its surroundings; suddenly it took to the air, floating almost like one of the squirrels, landed on a log house and was gone again. Possibly I had rescued it from one death only to have delivered it over to another. Other squirrels, and chipmunks, would kill it. I had no proof that flying squirrels would be any more tolerant.

That night I had my usual half hour of fun in the cage, handing out nuts, letting the squirrels crawl up my arm to sit on my shoulder or the top of my head, pretending not to notice when they stole nuts from my pocket—then foolishly stored them in the other pocket—but all the while I was looking for a wisp of gray and white that would be the deer mouse. I did not see it, that night or the next or the next, and sadly concluded the squirrels must have killed it. But about a week later I was amazed and delighted to see a squirrel pop out of an apartment doorway, then another squirrel, then a little gray-and-white head with pointed nose and beady eyes and ears like the petals of a flower. The mouse was not only living at peace with the squirrels but had become one of them. Although he was of a different color and another race, no doubt spoke a language foreign to them, he had been accepted as a member of their community, to share their bed and board.

The cage is weather-worn with age now. In summer it has been full of play, tawny bodies flitting from one end to the other; in winter, as still as the snow that covers everything. Then the log houses were silent also, but delicate traceries in the snow told a story. Close to the edge of the cage were the almost undiscernible tracks of the deer mouse, going once around in his nightly constitutional; here and there the larger tracks of the squirrels, stopping at the feeding dish or the peanut butter jar, pausing again at a place where a depression in the snow showed that some had been sucked up to quench thirst. And upon returning, all these tracks converged at the entrance to the community hall. Inside, where there was room for all, they lived now as one body, heartbeat close to heartbeat, breath upon breath; with little movement, only the readjustment of some part of the body for more comfort, the detachment of a segment for a short trip into the snow, they slept patiently, waiting for the warm nights of spring that would separate and make them many again.

Then there would be the return to last summer's apartments, 105 housecleaning, lining nests with fresh white cotton, quiet, casual matings, and afterwards, hours and hours, nights and nights stretching far into the summer's infinity, of little else but play. For the squirrels, this seemed the primary purpose of life. All else, obtaining suitable living quarters, making the nest, even reproduction that in most species seems to be the sole reason for existence—all these were tiresome chores that had to be got through as quickly as possible so that more time might be devoted to play.

For only one of them was life different, the largest of the males, who seemed to act as patriarch of the clan. Upon his shoulders, a trifle stronger than the rest, fell responsibility for the welfare of the community. When I put cotton on the shelf the squirrels flitted past it, too busy enjoying summer to think of winter's cold, all but the patriarch. He gathered up the cotton, stuffed it into his mouth and, half blinded by its bulk, went from apartment to apartment, peering in doorways. Who needed it most? Having made up his mind, he stuffed the cotton through an opening, pushed with his nose, his feet, his whole body until it was well inside, then hurried off to another of his chores.

One apartment had been set aside as a community storehouse, and into this the patriarch put all the nuts he was given, could find or, in an attack of zeal, could snatch from the very mouths of other squirrels nibbling on them. They were so careless! Half a nut was eaten, the rest tossed away. The patriarch watched it fall, jumped down to retrieve it, carried it to the storehouse, then went on a tour of inspection to make sure no other edibles had been discarded. He had no time for play. Often I wondered when he ate, and sometimes I felt sorry for him.

One day I passed the cage, caught sight of something moving, went in and found a baby, blind and helpless, lying on the floor. There was no way of telling which apartment it had fallen from; I chose at random and placed the baby in a doorway. It teetered for a moment, then an arm reached out, encircled it and pulled it out of sight. Either I had picked the right apartment or babies were also community property.

Sometimes I would see a squirrel that had grown feeble, from old age or sickness, hunched in a corner of the cage. Among most animals of the woods, the barnyard too, it is the custom for healthy members of the group to speed the departure of the dying. The dispatch, possibly merciful, is nevertheless a terrible and revolting thing to witness. The squirrels were different. They are a gentle people.

When one of them fell ill, when his eyes had grown dim, his body thin and slow to move, by common agreement, it seemed, he was allotted a certain portion of the cage. There he might sit in peace and look inward. All about him was busy, ceaseless careless, tireless activity: squirrels leaping, scrambling, flying, chattering, chewing. In his corner there was no movement, no sound, only the silent invisible drama of a small life ebbing.

When finally he stayed curled up in his nest, heart no longer beating, eyes open without seeing, the others removed his body, carried it down to the floor of the cage, where they placed it in a corner and covered it with whatever was at hand, leaves or discarded bedding or bits of nutshells heaped over it. That was how I found it and knew one of my friends was gone.

I had thought the squirrels were entirely safe in the cage, that nothing whatever could harm them; but nature in one of her schizophrenic fits of destruction cannot be outwitted or contained. When I found one squirrel after another dead, and not even properly buried, I was not only saddened but baffled. What was wrong? Had I neglected to give them some food they needed? Their diet was so varied; how could that be the cause? Then one bright sunny morning when I just happened to be near the cage, a bee zoomed past, lit on the wire and squeezed through, flew to a log house and entered. There was the answer. Bees had swarmed in the cage, dispossessed the squirrels, killed those that tried to resist.

Clad in thick slacks, heavy coat, high rubber boots, work gloves, a curtain snatched from the window over my head, I fought nature, bitterly and with a ruthlessness to match hers. Nevertheless, when I pulled apart the comb and saw all the helpless baby bees, I felt a remorse alien to her, and killed them with heavy heart.

The mouse was gone, and all but four of the squirrels. These four still live in an overabundance of apartments, and at present have as companion a little white mouse, so tiny that I wonder they have not mistaken her for a moth, a gustatory delicacy. This mouse, mother of many, had belonged to a child living down the road. One day they all escaped from their cage, the child's mother put out poison, the sole survivor was brought, in small desperate sorrow, to sanctuary in the squirrel cage.

She is a canny mite; she watches a squirrel store a nut, and as soon as his back is turned transfers it to her own storehouse, where most likely it is found later by the squirrel and repossessed; she is also graciously friendly. You would not expect a creature so minute to be drawn toward or even aware of anything as enormous as a human being; but each night when I enter the cage she meets me, to permit her fragility to be touched, gingerly, by a huge finger.

Somewhere there must be a hole in the wire big enough to permit her passage, and shortly after her arrival she was tempted to sample freedom. That night I caught sight of her flitting, like a moth, around and around the cage, searching for the way back in. I left the door open a crack. The next night she was back, and never again has she strayed through the hole in the wire. Having tasted freedom, she chose security. Given opportunity, perhaps the squirrels would make the same choice. Perhaps I did no wrong when, long ago, I set the trap on the box where we fed the birds.

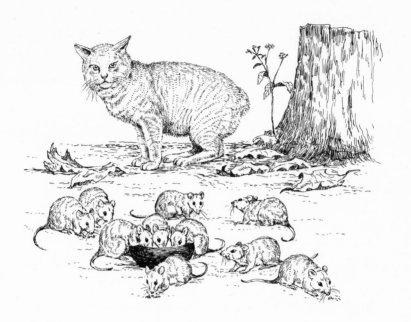

If I had not spent so much time out of doors, with the raccoons, the skunks, the squirrels, or just sitting, I might never have known Bobs. The first time I became aware of him, I was standing near the tree where I had watched the squirrels play. No doubt he, too, had watched them, but for a different reason.

I felt him before I saw him. Sometimes it is like that; I stand in the night, and know I am not alone. My surveillant may be only a deer mouse, staring down with fascination and uncertainty from the branch of a hemlock tree, or a screech owl, head cocked at a ludicrous angle, as if it had been pasted on wrong. This time, the beam my flashlight played in a circle around me was reflected in a pair of round eyes.

He was some distance away, a shimmering phantom that looked like a cat but was too large to be one, and as he turned I noticed he had no tail. Then he was gone. I went into the house and told Eric I might have seen a young bobcat.

The next night, again, I felt myself being watched. The stars were bright in a clear sky, and when my eyes had adjusted to their light I saw him, a dim shadow pacing warily around me. I switched on the flashlight to get a better look, caught again the gleam of eyes and shimmer of light fur; then where he had been there was nothing.

The following evening I put down a plate of cat food near the tree. He did not take it. The night after, I tried raw meat and that he ate.

For many nights thereafter I sat on the steps, not moving even when mosquitoes found and feasted on me. At last a shadow would come out of the deeper shadows of the woods, approach the plate of meat, pause to stare at the place where I sat; then I'd hear his lips smacking as he ate.

Gradually the waiting time shortened, until he came immediately, as soon as I had settled on the steps. That was my cue to move, each night a little closer to the dish. The first time I sat near enough to touch it he was uneasy, stood for a long while studying me; but finally he ate and, after one more puzzled look at me, slipped away.

The following night I extended my arm full length and touched the plate with one finger. This was a difficult pose to maintain and I was grateful when he came, belly low, ready for instant flight. He sniffed at the meat, at my finger, at the meat again, and ate. After that, for several nights, I put my whole hand on the plate, palm up, and when this no longer disturbed him, took the plate away and placed the meat on my hand. As he nosed over the fingers, palm, wrist, his whiskers sent almost painful chills up my arm; but he ate with great care, as if aware of my vulnerability.

The next step was crucial. As soon as he had taken his last bite, while he was still chewing, I turned over the hand that had fed him to touch the top of his head. The first few times he ducked and ran; at last he allowed me to stroke him, just between the ears, on the back of his neck, gradually farther and farther down his back, until I could slip the hand under his belly.

From then on I practiced lifting him, an inch off the ground, half a foot, a foot, and finally dared to pick him up. On my lap he purred; we were friends.

We had become acquainted in the dark, with only the light of the stars to see by. Now that I had his trust I carried him to the window for a better look; he was honey-colored, with slightly
darker stripes that shaded to lavender on the top of his head,

larger than a house cat, with broad, powerful shoulders, but not a bobcat. He was a Manx.

Where this breed of cat originated, no one really knows. There is a legend that when warriors took to wearing cats' tails on their helmets, the cats put a stop to such practice by growing no more tails. Another story says this cat was the last of all to board the Ark, and Noah, being in a hurry, clipped off the tail when he shut the door. Again, it is said tailless cats were aboard the Spanish Armada, and when one of the ships was wrecked near the Isle of Man, a pair swam ashore, where they flourished and multiplied. But the only certainty is that the Manx cat is now native to the Isle of Man.

In the early eighteen-hundreds, the sailor sons of a New Jersey farmer brought some of the Manx to this country, where the cats produced offspring, some of which "went wild." Now, about a hundred and fifty years later, clans of wild Manx are scattered throughout the woods of New Jersey and New York, and from one of them Bobs must have come, a product of many generations that had lived apart from man.

Where he spent his days we never knew, but after he was tame he posted himself each night on our back stairs, to guard them until dawn. Whenever we opened the door he would at once stand at attention, and wherever I went out of doors he followed —until I entered a building. He would not accompany me into the barn, the hay shed, or the house, all of which he must have suspected were enormous traps. As long as the weather was good we didn't mind his keeping vigil on the steps, but to see him squatting there in a pelting rain distressed us. And what of the snows to come?

I told Eric I thought Bobs trusted me enough; I would hollow out a bed for him in the hay shed, put down some blankets, and if I carried him there, surely he would not object? In a cold, miserable drizzle he walked with me as far as the door of the shed; I spread the blankets, went out again and picked him up. He purred as always until we were through the doorway, then made no sound at all, but suddenly gripped my head between his forelegs with surprising strength, like a vise, and dug his claws into my scalp. Had I cried out he surely would have mauled me, but I also made no sound, only turned and walked out again. Back in the rain he withdrew the claws, let go of my head, and a moment later he was purring. Quite simply, his devotion to me was not strong enough to overcome his fear of traps.

Some years before, Bert had pressed upon us several wooden barrels; we hadn't dared throw them away but never could think of a way they might be used. For a long time they had been stored in the barn, obstacles to skirt, rolling hazards to dodge; but as I tripped over one I suddenly had an idea. Couldn't we waterproof a barrel, and wire it to the top step, so it wouldn't fall off? At least Bobs could have that shelter when it rained. Eric was dubious, but the whole of the next day I worked on the barrel, coating it outside, lining it inside, wiring it to the step. Just before dark I put a blanket in it, and some raw meat—the only thing Bobs would eat—far back, so that he would have to go all the way in to get it. I was rather pleased with his little house, and hoped he would be.

A light rain started falling just as he came from the woods, making me even more certain that he would appreciate the barrel's shelter. He sniffed at it, backed away suspiciously, and went over to the other end of the steps to squat. I put my hand in the barrel, took out the meat, let him smell it, then put it back in the barrel. He blinked and hunched down under the rain.

Eric joined us, and after some deep thought said, "We could shove him in the barrel and clap a board over it. If he had to stay in for a while he'd get used to it."

This time I was dubious, but Eric trudged around in the rain hunting for a suitable board, and I felt honor bound to try his scheme.

"He knows you better," Eric said, "You put him in. I'll have the board ready."

I picked up Bobs, held him on my lap for a moment to reassure him, then in one quick movement popped him into the barrel. What went wrong, or exactly what did happen, we never knew. All we could remember afterward was sudden, violent turmoil, the barrel, the board, the two of us and Bobs all mixed up in such clattering confusion that I myself wasn't even aware of pain. Then Bobs was standing some distance away, looking hurt and bewildered; Eric with bleeding hands thrust out was staring aghast at my face; and I was trying to catch the blood trickling down from a deep gash in my lower lip.

"I guess he doesn't like it," Eric said, with such anti-climactic mildness that we both had to laugh.

After we were cleaned up and patched we went out again. While I apologized and fed Bobs, Eric removed the offensive barrel from the steps, and we were just where we had been.

The rain ended, the weather turned cold, a few days later the first snow fell. Eric and I took turns sitting on the back steps, holding Bobs to warm him, but we knew we couldn't keep that up. One night, after my turn, I stood over the stove and wailed, "I can't stand it. Not so much the cold, but feeling him shivering."

Eric was staring at the ceiling, where a cobweb waved at him.

"We could use a back porch anyway," he said dreamily. "I could build one."

"With what?" I wanted to know.

"There's a man wants to get rid of a chicken house. I could tear it down."

Although he was no mechanic, he was good at tearing down; nevertheless the chicken house took two days, and after the boards had been delivered, another two days were spent pulling out nails, an unpleasant, time-consuming job. But at last Eric was happily engaged measuring, sawing, hammering, and I removed myself from the vicinity; to watch was almost painful. But at least the porch was psychologically well built. The roof came first, to give Bobs shelter; the floor started at the outer edge and approached the house slowly, board by board, to become familiar and accepted before the old steps were removed; the walls went a little higher each day. When they reached the roof Bobs entered through the door without hesitation. Having watched this enclosure grow, he did not mistrust it as a trap.

Rain and snow sifted through where the roof of the porch met the house, the floor bounced alarmingly underfoot, wind whistled through nail holes and cracks, but Eric's masterpiece, which came to be known as the Accident, served its purpose. Bobs had a home, and we were content, or almost. The floor was icy cold, sometimes drifted over with snow, and Bobs still shivered.

"I could make him a dog house," I said. Borrowing some of Eric's astuteness, I put down a platform first, with a blanket on it, gave it one side, and another, until all four were up, with a hole cut in the last. Bobs learned to go through the hole, to lie on the blanket. Then came the top, detachable, in case he objected to it; but he didn't. Was he warm enough? I put my hand in to stroke him, felt the vibration of his purring, but also a draft. This brought out the sewing machine, to make a pair of curtains for his doorway. The first day they were hung wide open, the second, partly closed, the third, entirely closed. I think they amused Bobs as much as they did Eric. I myself never tired of watching him nudge against the folds to locate the part, nor of taking pride in the way they fell shut after his round rump had passed through.

Toward the rest of our cats he was gravely amiable, with special fervor bestowed on the little female Kate; and when she presented him with kittens sixty-three days later he did not try to kill them as a domestic tom might have done, but gave his off-spring all the fatherly concern and indulgence of the wild animal. However, no strange cat, or dog of any size, was allowed to set foot upon our land. Even some humans did so at their peril.

One day I glanced out of the window and caught sight of a man, a neighbor I did not particularly like, standing stock still on our path, about halfway to the house. Why was he just stand-ing there, and what had put that look of fear on his face? The answer was Bobs, stalking in a menacing circle around him, gradually closing in, in appearance so wild that I shared the man's concern. I hurried out.

"Call him off," the man said, hardly moving his lips. "He's going to spring."

"Bobs," I said, and at once a tame cat came to me, turning only once to give the man a last long look of hatred. In my arms he purred, and we watched the man lope off, his mind changed about paying a visit. Later this man was caught poisoning cats. Was Bobs aware of this evil, did he smell it on the man, or had he merely sensed and duplicated my own dislike? I could not know, but at least the man never tried to come back. Perhaps, facing Bobs, he had smelled his own evil.

Apart from the job of keeping off tresspassers, Bobs had other duties. Twice a day, in morning and evening, he helped me with the chores. Whenever the weather was favorable, one or two of the other cats might follow as I made the rounds, but Bobs did not follow; he led. When fresh snow lay on the ground he broke trail for me, not I for him. From rabbit cage to squirrel cage to the water hole to the hay shed to the barn—he knew the way better than I. With my thoughts on other matters, too often I had had to retrace my steps, either because I had forgotten something or because I wasn't sure whether I'd forgotten or not. Now, with Bobs for company, such uncertainty was eliminated. As long as I did each chore properly he trotted ahead, glancing over his shoulder occasionally to make sure I was coming along; if I deviated from customary routine anywhere, in any way, he barred the way. At first I did not understand and simply stepped over him; swiftly he would circle around to stop me again. Once I had caught on, we had an easier time; "What have I forgotten?" I'd say, returning mentally over our route. "Ah, yes!" And Bobs, knowing I was back on the track, would come as close to dancing as dignity allowed. During the first weeks of Eric's illness, when I dreamed a nightmare instead of living, I don't know how I'd have managed without him. Then he was truly my guide; blindly I followed.

Like the proverbial postman, he was deterred from making the appointed rounds by neither rain nor snow, nor wind nor even my remoteness. During a violent storm that drove rain straight across instead of down, I begged him to stay home; he would not. After we had done only half the chores I took him back and put him in his house; at once he was out, looking irked, to lead the way through the rain to where we had left off.

Only on rare occasions did he desert me, and then gave fair warning. Whenever he ate the half pound of meat that was his daily ration and asked for more, until he had had almost a pound, I would go indoors and tell Eric, "We're going to have a snowstorm. Bobs is leaving."

He never went away before the light falls, only when we were due for several feet or more. Somewhere he must have had a cave or burrow, and a remnant of wild instinct told him he must hole up there. As soon as the snow stopped he was back, breaking trail for me. Why snow made him depart, and never rain, is a question only nature could answer.

In the early days of our friendship he had brought me many gifts: shrews, mice, moles, woodrats, chipmunks, squirrels, once in a while a young rabbit. Usually they were dead, but in his eagerness to give he sometimes did not kill, and because this pleased me more, he came to know I preferred the quick to the 115 dead. Then our house had frequent and varied guests, caged overnight, released in the morning.

While we were going around a chipmunk might taunt him from a rock, or a mouse rustle in the grass at the edge of our path. His ears would go forward, his tailless rump wriggle in preparation for the capturing leap; I'd say "No, Bobs," and he would turn away, averting even his eyes from temptation. Always anxious to please, he soon had learned another lesson, that I disapproved not only of killing, but also catching. In fact, this lesson he learned entirely too well.

Just after I had put down his dish of expensive raw beef and gone indoors one evening, I glanced out of the back window and could not believe what I saw. This was in the fall of the year, when woodrats were coming to find winter quarters near an assured supply of food. In defense of our lean pocketbook we kept edibles out of their reach, except for the Whoever donation; now Bobs was making a much finer contribution of his own. Just as he took his first bite, a pair of black eyes peered around a corner of the porch, and a big woodrat nipped over to join Bobs, who looked up, slowly chewed and swallowed, and gravely backed away to give the rat precedence. Another pair of eyes appeared, another rat came to dine, and at last there were about fifteen in a circle around the food. Bobs stood near, looking on with almost paternal interest while they gobbled up his meat, even somewhat distressed when they squealed and fought over the last crumbs. Then he washed the memory of the one bite from his face while they, gathered around him, washed satisfaction from theirs. How often had he gone hungry because I had taught him not to kill? And how could I make sure he, not the rats, got his dinner?

I tried sitting with him while he ate. The rats, sure of welcome and grown overbold, looked upon me as no more than a harmless companion to the cat. I had to wave my arms and shout at them, even throw things. This disturbed Bobs so that he couldn't eat. Finally I went back to the way he had been fed in the beginning, offering the meat in my hand, which the rats didn't quite dare approach. By the time discouragement made them stay away, Bobs had become so accustomed to eating from my hand that he refused to have his dinner any other way. During the fall I found this a not unpleasant chore; in winter, torturous. Bundled in jacket, muffler, cap and boots, I sat beside him, offering meat as required, in bits no bigger than my thumbnail, warming freezing fingers inside my coat while he chewed. I think he spent so much time chewing not out of concern for my fingers, but because he wanted to keep me with him as long as possible.

Three years he was with us, a partner so unfailing that I took him for granted. But in the fall of the third year, when he was in his prime, a big fellow with powerful muscles and thick, gleaming coat, I somehow became acutely aware of the fact that he was, like all of us, mortal. He showed no sign of illness; his eyes were bright and clear; his appetite was excellent. Yet often, after he had finished eating, I took him on my lap to examine him closely, filled with strange, persistent foreboding that soon he would be gone. I tried to memorize every detail of his beauty, stroked him often so that I should not forget how he felt under my hand, tricked him into posing for a few pictures. He feared the camera as if it were a gun, but I hid it under my coat, snapped hastily and hid it again. The pictures didn't turn out well; my farewell pictures never do.

As the days grew shorter I spent more and more time with him, making sure he did not go out on the road or too far into the woods, all the time knowing this would only make the hurt that much greater when he left. Shortly before hunting season I built a cage, with wire walls so that he would not feel confined, and put his little hut in it, with the blanket that was familiar to him. Because he had watched while the cage was being built, he had no fear of it; there he stayed each day, curled up on his blanket, until the hunters left the woods at sundown. Then he did the chores with me and enjoyed freedom until just before I went to bed, when I fed him and put him back in the cage.

I found it difficult to make the morning rounds without him. Everything went topsy-turvy, and I could not shake off a feeling of sadness and loss, as if he had already gone. But in the evening we made up for the dreariness of the day. Never before had I seen him play; now his customary gravity was flung to the wind that chased dry leaves across our path. Having made sure I was proceeding in the right direction, he would deviate to cut a caper, pursue a phantom up the trunk of a tree or roll over with a captured stone hugged to his belly, back legs kicking it into pretended resistance. Yet no matter how preoccupied he seemed to be, the game was instantly abandoned when one chore was done and it was time to guide me to another.

I never knew what he did after I went indoors, and had misgivings that he might not return to be put back into his cage. But night after night when I called there would be instantly a rustling in the dry leaves, and I would see his light coat shimmering as he came to me from the dark woods. I held him on my lap while I fed him, and for a while afterward, until I could no longer bear the cold creeping inside my jacket; then side by side we walked to the cage, he hopped in, I closed the door.

I counted down the days of the hunting season, from fifteen to five ... four ... three ... two, and with each one ticked off, complacency grew. My hunch had been wrong. Bobs would not leave.

Two days before the end of the season, Kate fell in love again and hung around his cage, crooning. These last two days, when game had grown wary and hunters desperate, were the most dangerous of all, and I knew if I let Bobs out he would take Kate off into the woods; he was a strict observer of proprieties. Even making his daily deposit had to be done in privacy, far away from the house. I didn't dare free him; instead I put Kate in the cage. There the two of them spent the afternoon in blissful communion, and when the day ended, I took Kate indoors. Bobs helped me with the chores as usual.

It had been a cold, gloomy day. While we were going around snow fell, not much, just a few flakes. I didn't worry about Bobs that evening, thinking his interest in Kate would keep him nearby, and preoccupied with something I was writing, I didn't go out now and then, as was my custom, to check on the weather. So I was totally unprepared for what I saw when at bedtime I went out to call Bobs.

It must have been snowing all evening. Over two feet lay on the ground and the air was heavy, almost solid, with still more falling, silently, steadily. This was a big storm, the kind that made Bobs hole up. If I had fed him right after we had finished the chores, as before the hunting season, he'd have given me warning, asking for double rations. Now it was too late. The expanse of white lay unbroken all around; nowhere could I find any tracks, or depressions where tracks might have been made earlier. I called, and the sound of my voice pressed close around me, muffled by the snow, as if I were shouting in a thick-walled prison. I waded through the snow to the cage. He was not there. I went to the road, calling. The spaced lamps glittered behind the white curtain, cast down wavering pools of light; no small shadow came plodding out of the dark to shimmer under them.

I blamed myself for not having fed and caged him earlier, for ignoring the warning of the east wind and those first few flakes of snow, for neglecting to go out all evening, for relaxing vigilance now, almost at the end. Twice more I went out and called, then sat on the porch for a while, trying to feel close to him wherever he was. "Stay there," I begged. "You must be hungry, but stay there. Don't try to come back until it is dark again."

The next morning the sun shone, the snow sparkled; a fine day, made for gayety. Far away children were shouting and laughing, and farther still, shots split the brittle air. I saw many bird and squirrel tracks all about the house, but none made by a cat. In wide loneliness I did the morning chores; in the evening I waited for him, with fear in the pit of my stomach, and finally made the rounds by flashlight, in the dark.

For a week I fed hope with reassurance: he had met up with another female; he had been injured, but not seriously, and as soon as his wounds had healed he would be back; he was, like other cats, capricious, and stayed away by whim. All this I knew to be false. For three whole years his devotion had been constant. Nevertheless each night I went out to sit on the porch, not calling, just waiting for him.

At last I heard what had happened. On that fine morning when the sun shone, birds and squirrels sported over the snow, children played and laughed, a boy from the village, wandering through the woods, had come upon some tracks, six in all, five made by heavy hunters' boots, the sixth by a deer, and accompanying these were bright red drops of blood. The boy recognized the deer imprints as those of a doe, and knew following might be dangerous; in such evil days his life could be considered of less value than the two-hundred-dollar fine the violators would have to pay if caught with a doe. But, curious and somewhat indignant, he walked the way the tracks went, through deep snow, up a hill, across a meadow, over a stone wall, into dense woods beyond. There, near a thicket, he found the doe, her body still warm.

Tracks showed the five hunters had gathered around her, then scattered, perhaps because they heard or saw the boy approaching, each pair of boots going in a different direction. A shot rang out, not too far away. The boy went toward the sound, through the woods, to the stone wall; and that was how he came upon Bobs, on the other side of the wall.

The cat must have made a fine target, leaping over the wall, outlined clear against the white snow, and I suppose firing at it made the hunter feel better about having had to give up the doe. What was one cat more or less in a world where even human life was cheap? What matter that this one had an appointment to keep?

Once more the chores went upside-down and I had to retrace many steps, to do what I had forgotten or make sure I had not forgotten; and I remembered too well, how he looked as he trotted solemnly ahead, how he felt under my hand, how he purred on my lap, love naked in his eyes. I didn't need the pictures.

Can we alter destiny; by will and endeavor steer our lives into courses and conclusions other than those assigned? At times, in paroxysms of positive thinking, I thrust out my chin to challenge and defy; again like an animal I bow my head under the lash of fate, accept to gain tranquility, and so perhaps come closer to obeying fundamental law.

Upon some animals, as upon some people, fate lavishes favors. The raccoon living with us now is in this select group. A defenseless baby, she is spared by the fox that kills others of her size. Snatched by the rain-maddened brook, she is tossed harmlessly ashore instead of downstream to death. She is incautious, but cars miss her on the road, heavy objects she pulls down land beside, not on her. She is foolish, choosing to sleep in a chest full of mothballs; stretching luck far beyond toleration, she actually eats some of the lethal balls and suffers not even an attack of indigestion, perhaps because immediately afterward she consumes almost half a box of baking soda. She is a chosen one.

Others, caught in a balancing swing away from beneficence, are chosen also, but for adversity. Look closely and you can see doom in their eyes. You cannot help them; freed of one misfortune, they will be set upon by another. On a rainy day last summer I tramped hours and hours through the woods to locate a trapped dog; a week after his release he tried to cross the road, was horribly maimed by a speeding car and had to be destroyed. Only in giving terminal freedom do we have undisputed power.

Such an unfavored animal was Ginky, the opossum.

As everyone knows, opossums are native to the south, where they are abundant. Active and therefore needing food the year round, not too well clad, with thin coats, naked ears and feet, they could not survive in our inhospitable mountains; so we thought, until someone here, and another there, was confounded by the size of the rat he spied, looked again and identified the creature as an opossum. How these vulnerable, defenseless southerners could get through winters of deep snow, thick ice, bitter cold, and high winds, from October until almost June, nobody could figure out; the fact was they had indeed drifted steadily northward and settled at last in our woods.

The infiltration was gradual. When a boy in a neighboring village trapped Ginky, opossums were still rare enough so that there was much talk of the catch, some of which I heard. The boy, I was told, planned to keep the strange animal for a few weeks to exhibit to the curious; then kill her and sell the hide, which was worth fifty cents. Responding to a preservatory reflex, I said, quite automatically, "Tell the boy I'll buy the whole live opossum."

That was how we acquired Ginky, for the sum of one dollar. She arrived in an old dirty fruit crate, a tired, sorry looking creature huddled in the far corner. The trap had caught her jaw; a deep gash under the chin had become infected, half of her lower teeth had been torn out, pus drained from her eyes. She was sparsely furred, thin, dirty, sick, terrified. What could we do with her?

The old chipmunk cage, rebuilt and renovated any number of times, was stored away just then, in the hay shed. We dragged it into the house but could find no space on the floor large enough to accommodate it, unless we were to trip over it every time we crossed the room. Finally I thought of the upper bunk, never used for sleeping, but a fine storage place for tools, coat hangers, cardboard boxes and anything else we had to get out of sight in a hurry before company arrived. We cleaned it off, and the cage fit perfectly.

I lined it with newspapers and, optimistically, put a pan of earth in one corner. When I reached into the fruit crate to transfer Ginky to this new home, she did not play possum, as these animals are supposed to do when frightened, but opened her mouth wide, giving me a good view of the teeth she had left—an opossum is well equipped with fifty—and from her throat issued a terrifying sound, a combination of growling and hissing that sent a chill down my spine. It seemed advisable to wear gloves.

After I had drawn them on I sat beside her, talking soothingly, letting her smell the gloves, then reached over her head to take hold of the back of her neck. Now I know better. The best way to handle an opossum is not to touch it at all; the next best way, to take hold of the tail and immediately swing the body as far away from yours as possibly. Let one of the burr-like paws so much as brush against your clothing, and you are in trouble. The paw snatches and clings, you try to loosen it and another paw catches hold, and while you work on that the tail wraps around your wrist, or a finger, or a button, or inserts itself into a pocket and gets a good grip there. Unwrap the tail and all four paws dig sharp, tenacious claws into your clothing or your flesh, whichever is handier.

Having been foolish enough to allow an opossum to get attached, about the only way you can get it off is to remove whatever clothing it is stuck to or, should this violate decorum, lie down and wait for it to crawl off. All this I learned by picking up Ginky. As I pulled and pried and unwound to no avail, she gradually climbed higher until, having reached the top of my head, she had no place else to go. With her tail wound tight around one ear and the sharp claws dug into my scalp, I was not only uncomfortable but nonplussed, until it occurred to me that I might stick my head into the cage. When I did so she slowly unfastened her various tentacles and transferred them to the wire.

We gave her milk, which she slurped noisily; then offered her samples of everything else in the house until we found out what she liked: cheese, bananas, apples, grapes, and, especially, raw meat. Opossums are said to be omnivorous, but even poor starved Ginky was choosy, rejecting all vegetables. She drank water in immense quantities, and eliminated quite properly in the pan of earth, once each day. On a definitive diet of cat food, milk, fruit, and cheese, she gained rapidly and grew a fine glossy new coat.

After we had become acquainted she turned out to be a trusting, sweet-tempered, humble creature, satisfied with little: a small space she could call home, an old rug to lie on, a bowl of water, whatever food we chose to give her, earth to cover her daily deposit. Everything else, the hands that stroked her, the friendly voices speaking to her and later, the short walks out of doors, that was luxury. She enjoyed them quietly, shyly, with a gleam of pleasure showing in her sad little eyes, but she could do without, if she had to. She never demanded.

The day after her arrival I was already her friend, allowed to scratch her belly and even put an exploratory finger into her pouch—that odd, soft abdominal sac in which the young live and nurse for two months after they are born. Whenever I took her out of the cage she rode contentedly on my shoulder to gaze with mild interest at her surroundings, touch noses with the inquisitive cats, and never again did she growl or hiss.

I made a rope harness for her to wear out of doors. Each day I slipped it over her head, put her stubby legs through the loops, clipped on the leash, and off we went to explore the woods. Soon I came to realize the harness and leash were not needed. She stayed close by my side, with no wish to wander off on her own. All I had to do was carry her out, bend over so that my shoulder touched the ground to disengage her, then walk. She would follow. Sometimes I sat on a rock and watched her waddle around, looking at everything with bright remote eyes that seemed to be not really seeing things, but rather looking inward; or next to the woodpile, where she enjoyed exploring the small caves between the logs. When she was tired she would tell me by putting her paws on my lap, asking to be carried back home.

Opossums are supposed to be very stupid. In intelligence tests they score low, way down at the bottom of the list. Ginky could not possibly comprehend anything so complex as a swinging door. But findings of the aloof, mechanical researcher or scientist are not necessarily the equivalent of supreme law. I like to make my own tests. So I took Ginky to the door, pushed her nose against it, as I had done with any number of cats, to show her how it worked. The cats had been widely variant in comprehension, some learning immediately, others having to be pushed through over and over, day after day. Oddly enough Ginky, the dimwit, needed only one lesson; thereafter she lumbered in and out as if swinging doors were part of every opossum's heritage.

Outside she never went far, even though the cats tried to lure her, nor did she stay long. Our house was her home, and she was uneasy away from my protective presence. Shortly after she had come to live with us all of her claws had fallen out, probably because her general condition was so poor; the toes bled, scabs sloughed off, and finally new claws began to grow in, but they were still too short and tender for tree climbing, which no doubt added to her timidity. But she did prefer the good earth under the trees to a shallow pan in a corner. Once a day she took a short walk for this purpose; and so she went to her death. When she had not returned by sundown we hunted for her, knowing she would not stay away of her own volition; the next day I came upon some shred of her hide, just in back of the house. Our neighborhood was plagued at that time by some killer dogs, owned, but not fed by a farmer up the road, so hunger-driven that they tore apart and ate even skunks, undeterred by the stench. No doubt they had made short work of the defenseless Ginky.

In the fall of that same year, fortunately while Eric was absent, a trapper telephoned to ask if I'd like an opossum; he had found one in a trap and didn't want to bother skinning her. Just about that time Eric really had put down his foot, probably because he almost never could put it down without stepping on something that shrieked, clawed, or bit him in the ankle. Definitely no more animals, he said. So I named the new opossum Dixie and hid her in the barn, unoccupied then because the goats were still in pasture. Every evening I sneaked out to give her food and water and hold her for a while. She was also miserable looking and smelled terrible. After she had lived in the barn for about a month the first snow fell, we had to bring the goats in from pasture, and I moved Dixie to the hay shed. Then not long after, this shelter had to be cleared out to make room for a new load of hay. She had to be shifted again, but where?

Secretly, while Eric was not around, I built a cage under my bed. When it was finished I put Dixie in it, and carried on as before. While Eric napped after dinner I fed her, held her for a while, and tried to locate the source of the evil smell which seemed to be growing stronger. Fortunately there were always a few warning rustles indicating that Eric was getting up. As soon as I heard them I popped Dixie back into her cage and pulled down the bed cover that hid it. If she made any sound at all during the evening, Eric naturally assumed one of the cats was playing there.

This arrangement worked out well enough until one evening Eric neglected to make the usual preliminary noises; he just got up. Dixie was in my arms. He passed by, glancing at me briefly, went on as if he had not noticed, then did a beautiful double take and grunted.

"Well, where have you been keeping that one?"

I told him, he grunted again, threaded his way through all the cats and sat down to give his typewriter an extra hard pounding. All that evening the air was a trifle thick with disapproval, but by the following morning Dixie had been accepted, and became a member of the family. She still slept in the cage under the bed, but was free to go about the house whenever she wished. The new freedom, however, did not improve her disposition, which was unpredictable, but almost always bad.

She was amiable enough toward the cats, even when they played with the tail that so entrancingly resembled a snake, but I had to be circumspect in approaching her, taking care not to let my fingers or nose come too close to the great mouth that was always opened wide.

Since she no longer needed to be kept hidden, I had time to examine her more carefully and discovered she was host to an enormous number of fleas, which probably accounted for her bad temper. I put flea powder on the list of things Eric was to pick up the next time he went shopping, and when it came dusted her thoroughly. Certainly, as the label claimed, the powder was excellent for fleas; with each application they multiplied, until it seemed there soon would be all fleas and no opossum.

Eric made another trip and bought flea soap, and that was
more beneficial. Every few days I dumped Dixie in the tub, made

a swift collar of lather to keep the fleas from traveling to her head, then soaped the whole body, making her so furious that she whipped around and around, snapping at my dodging hands; I had to be quick indeed to keep away from those great jaws. But rage changed to terror when I poured in the water. Desperately she circled the tub, trying to scale its smooth sides; she sank resignedly, leaving countless fleas on the surface, blew bubbles under water, rose to the surface again and started paddling. So she learned to swim, and came to enjoy it; from one end of the tub to the other she plowed smoothly, making the turns with quite a flourish.

While I was drying her one day my finger accidentally caught in her pouch, and at last I found the reason why she smelled so. Having explored the placid Ginky's, I knew what a pouch should feel like, soft, clean membrane, with two rows of tiny milk glands lined along the back. Dixie's was full of matted fur. When she was trapped she must have been carrying young, which had died either then or later and disintegrated. I cleaned out the sac, but by then it was badly infected and needed daily treatment.

Dixie responded to my ministrations with anything but gratitude. Whenever I approached she backed into a corner to hiss, and while I worked on the pouch she tried her best to get at my hands. I knew it was just a matter of time; sooner or later she would succeed. It is best to come upon an opossum from the rear, but she made that impossible by backing into the corner. I had to attract her attention with one hand, then swiftly pass the other over her head and seize her by the scruff of the neck. Once I was not quite swift enough. Her head shot up, her huge mouth snapped shut on my wrist.

I had been bitten before, often, by dogs, cats, skunks, raccoons, chipmunks, rats, squirrels, mice, and goats, but never so painfully as this. Most animals, having bitten, let go. Dixie's jaws stayed clamped, like a powerful vise; I had a hard time prying them open. Then, too, fifty teeth can make an awful lot of punctures. Luckily those I got just missed the larger blood vessels, caused no particular trouble and healed readily. The primary injury had been to my feelings.

By the time spring came, Dixie was well enough to go outside. I can't say I took her for walks; she took me. Wherever she led, 127

I followed, until I felt we had been out long enough. Then I grabbed her tail, slung her over my shoulder, discouraged her attempts to sample an ear or my nose, and carried her indoors. At first her excursions were aimless, but eventually she found a place she liked, on the steep upper bank of the brook, and made for it every day, to grub in the earth beside a hemlock tree. After a while I saw she was digging a tunnel, which became deeper and deeper, until she could go so far in that I could not reach her. There she stayed. I coaxed and called and even put down food; her head would poke out to stare at me briefly, then vanish. Finally I gave up and went indoors without her.

That evening I saw her eating the food, but when I came near she scuttled back into the tunnel. She had no love for me, the baths, or the swabbings I gave her pouch. During the weeks that followed I worried a bit about the pouch, the possibility of her encountering dogs or other predators, and how she would get through the cold fall rains, the deep winter snow. Every evening I left food near her tunnel and she ate it, or somebody did. Once more just before the first snow I saw her. She had lost most of her fur, looked miserable, but still she preferred her cold, damp tunnel to my company.

By spring I had put her out of mind; then one night I went outside and there she was, smugly healthy, nicely rounded and wearing a fine new coat. I spoke her name and she hesitated, as if the sound evoked memories that were not entirely unpleasant; then she slipped under the rabbit cage and I never saw her again. Late in the fall, however, I found on the back porch a remembrance of her, a tiny baby opossum, just sitting there, as if waiting for me to come and get him. Like almost everyone else at that time, I had the flu and was feeling miserable. Groggily I stooped to touch him, said "hello, Dixie Boy," and picked him up. In the house I put him on the floor, he scuttled at once into the cave under my bed, where once his mother had lived, and that was the last I saw of him for two months. In the far corner was a box with a blanket in it, left over from Cricket's last accouchment, which had high sides, so that I could not see into it. Once in a while I swept and mopped under the bed, but took care not to disturb the box.

Each night, after I had got into bed and turned out the light, there would be sounds of activity below, snorts and sneezes, some bumping I finally decided must be Dixie Boy scratching himself, then the rasping of claws on the side of the box, and a plop. A moment later I'd hear the tap, tap, tap of claws going across the room.

Invariably he went first to the cats' pan, where there would be a rustling around and around, a long silence, and finally much scratching. Then he would tap back across the room, to smack his lips over the plate of cat food left in the corner, and after that to the water bowl, to conclude his feast with noisy and lengthy slurping. What he did after that I never knew; about then I always fell asleep.

This was the winter when Eric was ill, a victim of cruel aphasia, robbed of all power to communicate, in both speech and writing. Each evening we played a game of Scrabble, which the doctor had recommended for therapy. Sitting at the table one night, waiting for Eric to make his move, I happened to glance toward my bed and saw the overhanging cover wavering and bulging; and slowly a very large head poked from under it. I stared aghast. Was this the tiny baby I had brought in only two months before?

Eric made his play, looked at me, followed my glance across the room, stared wide-eyed; then, speechless, turned the stare accusingly upon me.

"But he was only a little thing when I found him," I protested.

Eric went on staring, but slowly the old grin came and spread, to be replaced before it was quite complete by a look of consternation. Prudently he lifted his feet off the floor. I felt like doing the same with mine, but couldn't seem to move. Here was a wild animal, a total stranger of fair size, right in our own house, rolling like a sailor straight across the room toward us. What would he do, and what should we do?

When he was almost at my feet he veered and shuffled away, then lifted his head, turned and shuffled back to sniff at my shoe; then in one long glide he shot back the way he had come and plunged under the bed.

After that, his brief exodus became a nightly ritual. We always had a snack while we played, and perhaps he was attracted by the smell of the food on the table. Once he had become familiar with my feet I ventured to speak to him, and this would send him 129 scuttling back under the bed, until the voice became familiar also. Then, as I spoke, I tossed him a piece of meat or cheese. Invariably and immediately there was a wild scramble; the cats, grouped around us in various attitudes of appeal, were experienced interceptors and usually snatched the gratuity while Dixie Boy, looking mildly dolorous, watched its consumption. However my aim gradually improved, Dixie Boy became more alert, and once in a while he managed to seize something from under the very nose of the nearest cat.

Soon he was looking at me with interest whenever he heard his name spoken, and I started feeding him by hand. The first few times he whuffed with fright, grabbed wildly, and I had to take care that my fingers did not become a part of his repast. But he was quick to learn the fingers were both friendly and vulnerable, and he found a way to accept food without doing them harm, by tilting his head sideways, so that the long canines were out of the way. I could offer him the smallest grape and he would take it gently.

One night he sauntered across the room with a mischievous glint in his eyes, quite casually nipped my ankle, and I knew we were at last firm friends. I thought it was time to try handling him, but he put an effective stop to that quite simply and harmlessly, by evacuating every time I tried to pick him up. However, he did allow me to stroke his head and scratch his back; as soon as I started scratching he would sag, evidently in transport, until he was squatting flat as a frog, and with ardor he would wash whatever happened to be in front of him, his own foot, the leg of a chair, my shoe, or if nothing else was there, the floor.

He began to awaken earlier, and sometimes was about in the middle of the day. No matter when, his first trip was to the cats' pan, where he left what seemed like a lake, and scratched with vigor. Then he replenished by slurping up an immense quantity of water, and just wandered around, never making a nuisance of himself or getting in the way, except when I mopped the floor. You'd hardly expect a great fat opossum to be playful, but he and the mop always had a wild game, fleeing and pursuing.

At five in the afternoon the cats were fed. I would blow one of those whistles that make no sound audible to the human ear but can be heard by animals at a considerable distance. From all directions the cats would come bounding to plunge through their door and gather around the food. Soon Dixie Boy responded to the whistle also and bustled over to join them. The males merely growled at him while they chewed, but the females took more decisive action, raking sharp claws over the opossum's nose. He would close his eyes, hunch up to take the punishment, and after the cats had got tired of swatting, inch closer to the dish, until one by one they sauntered away, saving face by pretending they weren't hungry after all.

When he had had his fill, Dixie Boy would retire to a corner to give himself a thorough cleaning, first his face, which he washed with both paws, like a chipmunk, then his pudgy body. For this he used his curiously shaped back foot, which had an opposing thumb much like ours. Wetting it with his tongue, he would send the foot in wide arcs over the fur, as if drawing circles in the air.

He seldom tried to climb up on anything but the shelf where we kept our canned goods. Whenever I caught him there I would give him a light slap on a padded buttock, and at once he would plop down to scuttle away; that is, until he came to rather like being patted. Then I had to resort to tweaking his tail, which seemed to be extraordinarily sensitive. After a few good yanks, he stopped trying to climb up on the shelf.

But later on, after we had retired, he simply had to get on the small table beside my bed, perhaps with an idea of joining me. True, I had shared my bed with others, a dog, any number of cats, a raccoon; once had even slept beside a goat, in the barn, when Sam was very ill. Nevertheless, I drew the line at an opossum. Repulsed, he always retaliated by knocking the clock on the floor and the telephone receiver off the hook. I think the operator must have got used to being awakened, or perhaps even stayed awake to wait for this nightly signal; immediately there would come over the wire the irritated crackling and tinkling of her displeasure. Each night I replaced the receiver, picked up the clock, and Dixie Boy, satisfied, laboriously climbed down and lumbered off to bed. He now had two retreats, the one under the bed and another in the wood box, no longer in use after our acquisition of the space heater; sometimes he slept in one, sometimes the other. This gave me a chance to clean whichever box he was not in; otherwise quite neat, he did have a bad habit of storing bones in his bed, where they moldered.

In February of that winter, a great storm buried us under fifteen feet of snow. For days nobody could go anywhere. Then the plows bustled along the road, cars moved again, and a man who lived down the road climbed over the snow mountain in front of our house to pay a visit. He was carrying a box, and I knew what that meant. "What's in it?" I asked immediately, but he was an orderly fellow and first had to tell his story.

Having crawled out of a window, he shoveled the snow away from his door, his car and his driveway, then while he was about it, thought he'd shovel a path to the trash basket and burn the rubbish that had accumulated during the storm. Just as he was touching a match to the heap, he noticed a piece of fur down near the bottom. Curious, he pulled it out, and found he had hold of an entire opossum. Right away, of course, he thought of me.

We opened the box and lifted out the little thing; it lay limp and clammy in my hands, just barely alive, its paws and ears fiery red. I stroked the belly and found a pouch. Yes, I told the man, I'd be glad to give her a home. Again Eric was away, once more hospitalized, but had he been home I knew he also would have given thought only to the miserable creature's need for help.

Not certain of how Dixie Boy would react, I didn't dare bring a second opossum into the house; she would have to stay on the porch, which had been glassed in and was fairly warm. I put a box in one corner, a bowl of bread and milk in another, a pan borrowed from the cats in a third. The opossum lay in the box just as I placed her, hardly breathing. I took her out again and for a long time held her in my arms, trying to give her warmth, wanting her to live not only because I preferred the quick to the dead, but also for another reason. If she survived, became acquainted with Dixie Boy and everything went well, I might be lucky enough to witness, perhaps even photograph, the birth of her young.

This takes place only thirteen days after conception, when the young are still only embryos, naked, blind, so tiny that about twenty would fit in a teaspoon, and just barely strong enough to crawl along a pathway licked smooth by the mother, up her belly and into her pouch. There they attach themselves to the nipples, usually thirteen in number, and hang on for dear life. Survival depends upon such tenacity, for nature, evidently particularly desirous of guaranteeing the continuity of this species, makes sure that many more are born than can be nourished, the number sometimes running as high as forty. The first thirteen to reach the pouch are the lucky ones. The rest die. For two months thereafter, those favored continue their embryonic existence; then, having acquired strength and vision and fur coats, they leave the pouch and crawl onto the mother's back, where they cling as she makes her nightly foraging tours. This was what I hoped to see.

The little female stirred in my arms, raised her head, tickled my chin and was promptly named Whiskers; hers were so long they seemed out of place, as if she had dressed up in mamma's to play at being grown up. I offered the bowl of bread and milk; she slurped and dripped. Then we went through the customary disentangling convolutions before she could be returned to the box.

The next day she was lively, snaking here and there to explore the porch, at every slight sound shooting back to her box like a torpedo. But whenever I held her she was quite amiable, at least toward certain portions of me. Like Gaul, I was divided into three parts. My feet she feared, my hands were suspect but tolerated, my head was her friend. As soon as I picked her up she wound her tail around my fingers, gripped my shoulder with her talons and snuggled her wet nose under my chin, her capacious and well-armed mouth uncomfortably close to the main artery in my neck; but she opened the mouth only occasionally, and then merely to yawn.

The talons were a problem. After she had sunk them into my flesh and held on so tenaciously that I couldn't pry her loose, I put on a heavy jacket before handling her. In time this jacket became an essential part of me; without it I lost my identity. When the weather turned warmer I sweltered and suffered, but if I switched to something lighter, she growled.

Each evening we made a tour of the house, Whiskers riding contentedly on my shoulder, then sat for a while in an armchair, where she never stirred except to touch noses with a cat, if one hopped on my lap to claim possession of me also. Sometimes, while holding Whiskers, I fell asleep; sometimes friends came to visit. She would stare mildly at the strangers, whiskers atremble, then burrow her head like a shy child under my protective chin. On our tour one evening we happened to pass a mirror and I held her close, wondering what she would think of herself, not expecting much of a reaction because she was supposed to be stupid. She took one look, snarled with rage and lunged at the mirror with such force that she almost broke it, along with some of her own teeth. The next night we stopped again before the mirror; no matter which way I turned, she turned her head the other way. Never again could she be persuaded to glance at her reflection.

After the tour and the conference in the armchair, we went back to the porch and I held her on my lap while she ate. Even a towel was insufficient protection; I should have worn a raincoat. She would have nothing but bread and milk, and unlike the fastidious Dixie Boy, was a very sloppy eater, fishing out bits of the soaked bread with her fingers to place them on my lap for consumption. I had started out wrong and was stuck with this procedure; she would not eat at all unless I held her.

She was also—I think willfully—very dirty. Instead of using the pan, she chose a corner. I moved the pan to that corner and she used the one from which it had been taken. I spread newspapers in all four corners; she used the middle of the floor. I laid newspapers over the entire floor, whereupon she decided the first corner was the one she preferred.

During her first few visits, Dixie Boy had slept unperturbed. But the scent of her must have wafted through his dreams; soon he awoke whenever I brought her in and paced the floor around my feet, lifting his nose to sniff questingly. Whiskers craned her neck to get a better look at him, then hid her head and clutched me tighter than ever, indicating she had no desire to meet him. For some time that was all that happened; then Dixie Boy acquired what seemed to be a kind of nervous tic. Every once in a while his lips would twitch and make a strange smacking sound. It worried me somewhat until I discovered these attacks always coincided with the entrance of Whiskers. Then he began having them before she came in, whenever I opened the door to the porch, and finally he started smacking as soon as he saw me walking toward the door. Evidently the sound was a mating call. For a dull-witted animal, he was uncommonly shrewd. I adhered to a pretty regular schedule, which he soon knew as well as I. When it was time to get Whiskers he was right there, racing me to the door, and whoever says opossums are sluggish has never tried outrunning one. To get enough of a handicap, often I had to make several false starts, and even so barely managed to close the door between us. One evening I didn't, quite. Dixie Boy shoved a powerful hook into the crack that remained, flung the door open and barged past, almost knocking me down. By now he was entirely too big to handle, with or without the threat of evacuation; and of course the two of them had to meet sometime, if Whiskers was to achieve fulfillment. I went into the house to get my camera, returned to post myself in what I hoped would be a neutral corner. Dixie Boy was standing in front of Whiskers' box, smacking invitingly; there was no response, until suddenly Whiskers' head shot out and from the cavern of her mouth came a mighty hiss. Taken by surprise, Dixie Boy cringed and backed away, still smacking, but dubiously. In the corner was a bowl of bread and milk, put there each day in the fond hope that Whiskers might eat without my attendance; he bumped into it and although he'd already had his dinner, started eating like mad, probably out of sheer nervousness. Whiskers watched a moment, black fury in her eyes, snaked out of the box, flung herself on him with a blood-chilling growl, caught him broadside to knock him off his feet, and clamped her jaws around the greater part of his neck. While I was climbing on a chair he squealed like a pig in a slaughterhouse, thrashed around and finally managed to shake her off, whereupon Whiskers, perverse as all females, began eating the food for the first time all by herself.

Dixie Boy had had enough; all he wanted was to get away. While her attention seemed to be on the food he tried to sneak past her to his own quarters in the house, but she was not that preoccupied. After him she went, snarling. He dove under the bed, into his box. She dove after him. Helpless, I stood by listening to the sounds of a terrible battle, squealing and grunting, thudding and thrashing, a great clatter as some paint cans stored under the bed were overturned; then they all came rolling out, the cans, Dixie Boy, and Whiskers.

He fled to the kitchen, she pursued. He climbed the forbidden 135 shelf of canned goods, she tried to pull him down. He lost his hold and fell, taking all the cans with him in a mighty crash, scudded and skittered through them as they rolled in every direction and sought sanctuary behind the stove, wedging himself into the small space between it and the wall. The slender Whiskers had no difficulty at all getting at him there. More squeals and grunts and thuds were accompanied by a most puzzling and disturbing clanking of metal, then Dixie Boy managed to extricate himself from the trap and shot across the room to his other home, the wood box. Whiskers was just dispossessing him there when I noticed a strong smell of kerosene seeping through the house and two sets of glistening wet footprints where the opossums had passed. I took a look and found a pool slowly spreading under the stove.

Dashing outside, I turned the cock, shutting off the flow of oil. Dashing inside, I bumped into Dixie Boy, thudding across the room again. Earlier, I had had one of my rare domestic turns and had done some ironing; the board was still there with the iron on it, the cord dangling down like a noose, and into it Dixie Boy's head went unerringly. I made a flying tackle, caught the iron just as it was slipping off the board, giving Dixie Boy such a scare that he doubled back to throw himself straight into the jaws of Whiskers, who shook him like a dustmop. Dancing around them, I finally saw a good opening, grabbed Whiskers by the tail, carried her snarling out to the porch and closed the door.

So ended the opossums' first evening together, for them but not for me. The next two hours I spent retrieving cans and putting them away, scraping up spilled paint, sopping up oil, mopping the floor; the following day, with pain, I handed out a check to pay for repairs to the stove.

But Dixie Boy and I were not discouraged; far from it. The next evening he was at his post near the door, smacking his lips again; and camera in hand, I opened it for him. This time the assignation was less violent. After a brief skirmish on her own grounds Whiskers slipped into the house and under the bed, with Dixie Boy in pursuit for a change. There followed some thumping and a few squawks, then all was quiet. When I poked my head under the bed half an hour later, Dixie Boy was curled up in his box, Whiskers crouched in a corner.

Their rapport continued until Whiskers showed evidence of being in what adults delicately refer to as an interesting condition and youngsters call pregnancy; then she was isolated on the porch again. With the growth in girth her amiability decreased. One evening while I held her she opened her mouth wide, but not to yawn. Fortunately her tail was coiled around my fingers; a swift yank combined with a quick turn of the head just saved my nose from having to be rebuilt by a plastic surgeon. After that there was always uneasiness between us, on my part because of the prominence and vulnerability of my nose, on hers because of the sensitivity of her tail. Quite simply, we no longer trusted each other.

At any time, the two opossums could have left the house through the swinging door, had they wished. Both seemed to prefer the luxury of confinement to the hazards of freedom, but when Whiskers' time came she must have felt the need for more privacy. Just as I had completed elaborate plans to photograph tiny baby opossums traveling up mamma's belly, I looked into her box and found it empty. She had not been gone long; her bed was still warm. Outside, I was just in time to see her long tail snaking around a corner of the house. I lunged to catch hold of it, missed, and gave her such a turn that she ran across the yard under the rabbit cage.

Sadly I put away the photographic equipment, but mixed in with disappointment was a certain relief. True, the porch had been spotless while Whiskers lived there, but I rather enjoyed being less closely affiliated with the mop. Dixie Boy had no such consolation. Although the opossum's brain is supposed to be too small and rudimentary to accommodate any but the most primitive emotions, I should say he grieved. For a whole week he would not eat. Again and again he begged to be let out on the porch; he would go to Whiskers' box hopefully, peek in, smacking his lips, his body swaying between aggression and timidity, daring her to come out and preparing for flight if she did. When she did not, he would snuffle around the porch, pausing at the swinging door, to gaze wistfully at the world beyond. I thought he might decide to join Whiskers out there, but in the end he always turned and went back into the house.

At last he found sufficient courage to enter the deserted box. 137

Inside he snuffed and scratched for quite some time. When he emerged he did not loiter but returned at once to his own quarters, and never again did he smack his lips, or ask to be let on the porch.

Our relationship was now so pleasant that I am tempted to say: if the ticking of your clock sounds lonely but you have neither the time nor the inclination to do much catering, get an opossum. Usually he joined me in the kitchen while I was preparing dinner, not getting underfoot like the cats, just sitting quietly in a corner doing his laundering. If the cats were not looking I would slip him a piece of meat or a bone, which was accepted with such gentleness that I thought I might try teaching him to sit up. Of course authorities would say that was impossible, but he comprehended immediately, only had difficulty balancing his rotund body on his hind legs. When he finally learned how to defy gravity, he made the performance routine. Once, in a hurry, I simply handed him a chunk of meat; he would not accept it, not until he had laboriously raised himself and tucked his paws neatly against his chest.

Early in October he started making a nest in the wood box. I had read about opossums using their tails for toting, but so much written about the opossum is apocryphal that I suspected this also was the product of someone's fertile imagination. Then, shortly after I had cleaned the cats' pans and filled them with torn paper, I heard Dixie Boy rustling there for such a long time that I looked to see what he was doing. Most of the paper had been taken out of the pans and piled neatly on the floor; some of it was stuffed, like a rosette, in his looped tail. For some reason my presence disconcerted him; he scuttled at once into his box, where he deposited his load and fussed long over it, spreading and tamping down the paper with his nose.

In no other way was he shy, but always when he caught me watching while he gathered nesting material, he stopped immediately. However, by pretending not to look, I could observe him from the corner of my eye. Having transferred all the paper from the pans to the heap on the floor, he would take one piece in his mouth, slip it into his right paw, pass it under his belly, and kick it with hind foot into the looped tail. This was done with great rapidity; while the back foot was kicking, the mouth was already picking up another piece.

When I tore up a brown grocery bag and put it with the rest of the paper, he carefully picked out these pieces, thus showing a preference for brown, the color of the dry leaves he would have gathered in the woods. After that I saved the grocery bags for him, and when there were enough, he remade his nest, discarding all the white paper.

As the weather grew colder he spent more and more time in his nest, but came out each evening to wait in the kitchen until he was asked to sit up for his tidbit. Later he ate with the cats, drank his enormous quantity of water, then retired again.

Toward the end of October we had a violent storm that piled snow in great drifts, uprooted trees and tore down all the utility wires on the road. Most of the day I spent outdoors, shoveling snow off the roofs; at twilight I came in to get dinner by candlelight. Because I was tired and the illumination was so poor, I didn't notice whether Dixie Boy was in his corner, nor whether he ate with the cats. I don't suppose it would have made any difference, but afterward the oversight was cause for some self-reproach.

When the cats had been fed and the dishes washed, I could think of nothing else to do in semidarkness, and went to bed, to fall asleep almost instantly and dream of wind-driven snow. Then the dream changed. I heard Dixie Boy's claws tapping over the floor, just as I had in those days when he was a wild creature living under my bed, and I said, out loud it seemed, "He's dying." But of course I had spoken only in the dream.

Some time later I was suddenly awakened by the sound of metal clanking, motors roaring, voices shouting on the road. I got up, started across the room, tripped over something soft, said "I'm sorry" to the cat I thought I had bumped into, and went to the window. On the road an eerie ballet was being performed; against brilliant weaving beams of light, shadows floated as in still another dream, dipping, rising, gliding, soaring. Repair men were replacing the broken wires. I watched fascinated, until suddenly, with a twinge of apprehension, I remembered the earlier dream, and the soft thing my toe had touched in the dark. I lit a candle, and there on the floor lay Dixie Boy, looking at peace and in good health, as if he were merely sleeping; but he was dead.

For the first and last time in his too short life I held him in my 139 arms, over sixteen pounds of ugliness and stupidity, a lowly creature of no discrimination I had come to respect, an unlovable oddity I had grown to love. Much time passed before I remembered not to glance toward the empty corner in the kitchen, where he had sat laundering his fur, waiting patiently for me to notice him.

Shortly after the big storm we had an equally impressive thaw, and once the flood waters had receded, Whiskers came back, or as nearly as she could. The front door was closed and she could not get through the swinging door, so she chose the next best shelter and crawled under the house. Puzzled by the sound of stones being flung against the steps, I went outside, just in time to see her rump and long tail ease into the tunnel she had dug. Through the rest of the winter she lived below us, in quarters at least dry and protected from the wind, perhaps even warmed slightly by our heat; and at least she never went to bed hungry. Whenever there was fresh snow I would see her tracks, like a row of little starfish, going to the plate of food I left near her tunnel and away again. During the following spring and summer, with no snow to read, I had no idea whether she was near or far, or even alive. Then one night in early fall I went outside, and stepped into the past. On the porch was Dixie Boy, a tiny fellow, just as when I had first seen him, waiting for me to come get him; only now he carried in his coiled tail a small bunch of autumn-tinted leaves, like a suitor's nosegay. I tried to think of another name, Whiskerson, perhaps, stooped down to touch him, then did not, quite. No, I thought, he would be better off in the hardship of the woods, where he would have to search for food and battle to survive. I offered a life too easy, too soft; that must have been why Dixie Boy died. And I turned away, leaving him there holding up his bouquet of bright-colored leaves.

I was mistaken. The subsequent winter turned out to be the brutal one in which birds dropped like stones from the trees, banished cats froze on doorsteps where they sought shelter, deer perished in the woods, and Abbie died. Since then I have seen no rows of dainty starfish in the snow, nor to my knowledge has anyone else on this mountaintop. Perhaps some time these foolish, trusting little marsupials will drift back again. If ever they do and my hand still can turn the knob, the door of this house will be open to them.

Since the soul is not an identifiable part of the human anatomy, its existence cannot be proved; nor is there any way to establish that animals do not have souls.

One day in early winter, when an unpleasant wet snow was packing deep slush on the ground, I happened to glance outside and saw a little boy standing before the house, gazing at it. He looked cold and forlorn, was obviously lost, but I could not take him in. I recognized him and knew him to be a wild creature; there was no telling what he might do to the other animals in the house. Yet I could not simply ignore him; he also had a heart that beat.

I put on jacket, cap and boots, went out to him and offered my hand, palm up, as one does to show an animal there is nothing to fear. "Come," I said. The place where he lived was quite far, about a mile away on another road. He backed off, staring at the hand, came closer hesitantly, his eyes going from the hand to my face and back again. "Come," I said, and with a grunt he surrendered; his hand crept into mine.

As we walked down the road I could feel the tremors shaking his frail body. He had on only a light jacket and soaked canvas shoes, but that was not the sole reason for his trembling; he was also afraid. Now and again he stopped to glance around wildly, looking for a place to run to, to hide; then, just as I had with others, I murmured encouragement, taking care not to look at him, only giving my voice and my hand, until he trusted again.

As we approached his own house children came spilling out, brothers and sisters sent to hunt for him. "Ah! Ah! Ah!" he cried to them, nodding at me and hopping up and down. "Ah! Ah!" In his eyes was the look I had come to know so well, and I had heard those sounds before also. "Look, look, look," they said. "I have found a friend!"

He did not want to let go. "Ah! Ah!" he cried as they tried to tear him away. And how often had I not heard that same wail issuing from an animal when a door was closed between us?

Not long after, the boy died, and he was given a good Christian burial. Did he have a soul? He walked upright, but otherwise bore little resemblance to man. With animals he had much in common: comprehension only of the reassuring voice and hand, expression only in sounds of pleasure or pain and the eloquence in his eyes. Where is the line drawn? Where does one begin, the other cease to be?

Once I asked a wise person about survival and received the reply, "All those who are loved live on." All. I like that. Somewhere are they waiting, Abbie, Muff, Gretel, Bobs, the squirrel that perched on my shoulder, the mouse that beat like a heart against the palm of my hand? All of them, and among them, Eric, surrounded by them, shaking his head reproachfully, but grinning to give the lie to disapproval?

Yes, I should like that. Meanwhile there are others, always others, coming to the upturned hand.

Notes about the Author

Mrs. Era Zistel Posselt is a resident of a small house in the woods, in Haines Falls, New York. She shares her room and board with the characters of this book—cats, goats, flying squirrels, chipmunks, raccoons, an occasional opossum, etcetera. Born in Cleveland, Ohio, she took her B.A. at Western Reserve University and came finally to New York City where she briefly pursued a career as a model, then as a writer. Eventually, weary of city life, she and her husband moved to upstate New York and began their life with the creatures from the woods.

Mrs. Posselt has written extensively about animals, both in magazines and in books, the most recent of which is *Wintertime Cat*. She is a writer of most professional skill, who is, moreover, able to convey to her readers her deep feelings about animals and about her life with them.